130 Fun Facts
From God's Wonder-Filled World

BERNADETTE McCARVER SNYDER

Illustrated by Chris Sharp

Liguori
LIGUORI, MISSOURI

Dedication

I dedicate this book to all my friends and family (especially my son, Matthew, and grandson, Will) who have helped me discover and enjoy the exciting and sometimes hilarious surprises in God's wonder-filled world—and who have taught me to take time to see the holy in the ho-hum.

Imprimi Potest:
Richard Thibodeau, C.Ss.R.
Provincial, Denver Province
The Redemptorists

Published by Liguori Publications
Liguori, Missouri
www.liguori.org
www.catholicbooksonline.com

Library of Congress Cataloging-in-Publication

Snyder, Bernadette McCarver.
    130 fun facts from God's wonder-filled world / Bernadette McCarver Snyder ; illustrated by Chris Sharp.—1st ed.
        p. cm.
    Summary: Presents, from a Christian perspective, miscellaneous facts and trivia about saints, smybols, human beings, animals, geography, history, and many other topics.
    ISBN 0-7648-0925-3 (pbk.)
    1. Christian children—Religious life—Miscellanea—Juvenile literature. 2. Christian life—Miscellanea—Juvenile literature. 3. Curiosities and wonders—Juvenile literature. [1. Christian life—Miscellanea. 2. Curiosities and wonders.] I. Title: One hundred and thirty fun facts from God's wonder-filled world. II. Title: One hundred thirty facts from God's wonder-filled world. III. Sharp, Chris, 1954–ill. IV. Title.

BV4571.3 .S59 2002
242'.62—dc21   2002073075

Printed in the United States of America
06 05 04 03 02   5 4 3 2 1
First edition

Contents

Introduction

What Is a "Heavenly" Fun Fact?

Some facts are regular…like your name, address, and phone number…and the fact that some boys collect coins and some girls ride bicycles.

Some facts are fun…like the fact that an elephant can't sneeze and there's a flower that eats bugs.

And some facts are "heavenly" like the fact that God made you AND also made lots of wonderful, wonder-filled things and put them in your world—so you can discover them and be surprised!

So open this book and enjoy all the different kinds of regular AND heavenly fun facts!

Could You Buy a Sandwich With a Sandwich Coin?

You sure could! For years, the government made coins out of silver, but then they decided they should start to make coins out of something else. In the 1960s, somebody discovered a way to make "sandwich coins" by putting pure copper on the inside (like bologna) and a copper-nickel mixture on the outside (like bread)! The coins still look like silver, but they're not!

Did you know there are all kinds of different coins made out of all kinds of different metals in all kinds of different countries? Some people like to collect different kinds of coins as a hobby. Some people collect coins until they get enough to buy a sandwich. And some people collect coins until they have $5 and then they give the $5 to the poor or send it to the missions. Which would you like to do? Maybe you could do all three!

Does a Dog Ever "See Red"— or Purple or Pink?

Did you know that when somebody gets really angry, people say "he sees red"—but no matter how mad a dog gets, he will NEVER see red! That's because dogs can't see any kind of color. Everything they see is gray. Apes and some monkeys, some birds and some fish, can see some colors but dogs and cats can't.

Aren't you glad God made your eyes so you CAN see colors? If you could only see gray, you wouldn't know that the American flag is red, white, and blue or a watermelon is red, white, and green! Tell God thanks today for the colorful world he painted for you.

Could I See Your License?

You probably don't have a driver's license yet—but you may have played the license game when you're riding in a car and you watch for out-of-state license plates and see who in the car can spot the most the fastest. Well now, that game can be even more fun since people can purchase license plates with messages on them. Have you seen some funny message license plates—like UGO2FAST….IM2TIRED… DONTBMAD… URAQT…DOUCMYRV.

What kind of license plate could you make that would be funny or just nice? You can only use 8 numbers or letters. How about BHAPPY…GOOD4U…PRAY4ME? Ask a friend to play the license-plate game with you and see how many messages you can make.

Did God Make Bubble Gum?

Well, not exactly—but it couldn't have been made without his help. You see, God made a tree called a sapodilla tree. It grows in the Yucatán forest and in Guatemala, and it is a special kind of tree. When you make a deep cut into one of these trees, a thick sticky fluid or "sap" oozes out. A long time ago, somebody found out that when you take some of this sap and boil it, it becomes elastic and then you can add sweetening and flavors to it—like cherry or cinnamon or mint—and turn it into chewing gum!

Somebody also figured out how to shape it into flat "sticks" of gum that could be wrapped and packaged and shipped to a store near you so you could buy some! God made the tree and a human figured out how to make the gum. Good things always happen when God and people work together!

Good things can happen to you too when you and God work together! What would you like to ask God to help you do today?

How Can You Tell a Crocodile From an Alligator?

Both of these scary-looking swimmers are in the same family but did you know you can tell the difference by looking at their nose-y snouts? (Only look at PICTURES of them though. You don't want to get too close to either one!)

God made the crocodile with a rounded snout and the alligator with a pointy one. Both of those snouts are full of dangerous sharp teeth but the round-nosed crocodile is grouchier and more likely to "pick a fight." When it's lunchtime today, pretend you're an alligator and chomp down on whatever lunch you're having—even if it isn't your favorite. But DON'T pretend to be a crocodile because nobody likes somebody who picks fights!

Mirror, Mirror Not on the Wall

Did you ever hear of the famous artist Leonardo da Vinci? He was an Italian genius who was an architect, an engineer, and a scientist, as well as a painter, sculptor, and teacher. And he kept many journals or notebooks filled with notes and drawings. One of his ideas was a plan for a helicopter a few hundred years before anyone else thought of one!

But Leonardo had a special trick. In some of his notebooks, he used a special "code." Some of the pages were written by hand BACKWARDS so no one could read them. Of course, the secret was that you COULD could read the notes if you held a mirror over the notebook!

Why don't you try that today? Write a letter to God, telling him all your secret thoughts—but write it backwards. Unless you tell the secret, no one will be able to read it except you and God!

What Is a Drupe?

Did you know that a fruit God made with a single seed or "pit" is called a drupe? The cherry, peach, apricot, and plum are all drupes! Do you like to eat any of the drupes? Do you have a favorite drupe? Drupes are good for you so if you ever have a day when you FEEL a little droopy, maybe you should eat a drupe and then you would feel better! Or maybe you could ask your mom or grandma to make you a sweet drupe pie. Mmmm…maybe cherry pie or peach pie, with a scoop of vanilla ice cream on top?

Elephant Calling!

Hello!

Did you know elephants don't need telephones? Why? Because God gave elephants ears that can hear so good, they can hear and send messages to other elephants that are as far away as seven miles! You might say that an elephant's ears work like the satellite dish some people put on a roof to pick up faraway TV signals!

In addition to those great floppy ears, the elephant has that long funny trunk. He uses it to drink and smell and make a loud "trumpet" noise. He uses it to pick up food and can pick up something as big as a tree or as small as a peanut! He also fills his trunk with water and gives himself a shower to cool off or sprays himself with dust to ward off insects.

And guess what the elephant does when his back itches? He picks up a big stick with his trunk and uses it as a back scratcher!

A mother elephant does all those things plus one more. She uses her trunk to pick up a small uprooted bush and uses it as a paddle to spank the baby elephants when they misbehave!

Do you think your friends know all those things about the way God made elephants? If they don't, you can tell them!

Who's Got the Palindrome?

You've probably heard of the Superdome and the Astrodome but do you know what a Palindrome is? And who has one—your mother, your father or maybe one of your friends? Well, a palindrome is a word, a number, or a sentence that is the same backward as it is forward. So your mother or father may have names that are palindromes—if you call them Mom or Dad! And maybe a friend has one if the friend's name is Bob or Nan… or if you have a silly friend who is a Kook!

Numbers can be palindromes too—like the year 1991 or the year 2002. And the next palindromic year will be 2112! How old will you be in the year 2112?

Sentences are trickier but they can be palindromes too. One of the best-known palindromic sentences might be what Adam said to Eve in the Garden of Eden: "Madam, I'm Adam."

Do you have a name that is a palindrome? Try to think of some palindrome names or words that are the same forward and backward…Lil, Sis, gag, deed, toot, peep. Then think of how nice it is that God knows you both backward and forward. He made you and he knows you and he loves you. Isn't that a WOW!

How Smart Are You?

Did you know that some of the best-educated people in the world live in Iceland? They must read lots of books because everyone who lives there is REQUIRED to get a good education. But that's not all—to get a job there, you have to know how to speak at least THREE languages.

How many languages do you know how to speak? If you wanted to learn a "foreign" language, which one would you choose—Spanish, French or Icelandic?

Isn't it nice to know that you can pray in ANY language and God will hear you—since He speaks them all!

Denise Denies That Cathy Is a Yacht!

Did you ever hear of anagrams? That's a fun game where you take a name or word and try to rearrange the letters to make a different word. Cathy can be changed to yacht. Denise can spell denies. Mary can become Army, sore can become rose, Clare can become clear, and bore can turn into robe.

Why don't you get a friend to play this game with you today? Get out a book and look at words and see how you can switch the letters to spell something different—like changing "words" to be "sword!"

With an anagram you can even change "evil" to "live" and that's great—get rid of the evil and live a good happy life!

What Did Mrs. Fillmore Do?

Back in the 1800s, a young lady named Miss Abigail Powers taught in a one-room schoolhouse in New York State. There was a young man named Millard who worked in the stony fields of his father's poor farm nine months of the year but came to study at Miss Abigail's school the other three months. She encouraged him to buy his first book—a dictionary. Then she helped him study to become a lawyer. And then they got married.

Years later, Millard Fillmore became the president of the United States and Miss Abigail—who was now Mrs. Fillmore—became the First Lady. When they moved into the White House, Abigail was surprised to find that there were NO BOOKS in the White House. She immediately fixed up one room with some bookshelves and asked Congress to give her $250 to buy some books. So what did Mrs. Fillmore do? She started the first White House library!

Do you like to have books to read in YOUR house? Do you like to go to the library to check out books? Who knows? If you keep reading and studying, maybe some day you might have your own library full of books—or you might live in the White House and read the books in that library!

How Old Can a Tree Be?

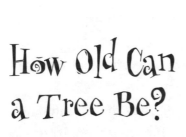

I n the forests of North America, some very special trees are growing, the oldest living trees in the world—the bristlecone pines. Some of them have lived to be almost 5,000 years old!

What's that you say? How does anyone know they are that old? Well, there's a special way of telling the age of a tree. In the tree's first year of life, the trunk of the tree develops a woody ring that grows around the pithy center of the trunk. Then every year, the tree adds another ring—just like you add another candle on your birthday cake. When the tree is cut down, you can cut a "slice" out of the trunk and count the rings and you'll know how old the tree is.

The bristlecone pine holds the record for being the oldest but there are other trees that have grown to be very old too: the sequoia, almost 4,000 years; the cypress, 3,000 years; the chestnut, 2,000 years; and the cedar of Lebanon, 1200 years.

It's a good thing God didn't make people to grow that old—they'd have to have an awful lot of birthday candles!

What Is a Saint?

Actually, there might be somebody you know who goes to your school who could grow up to become a saint because a saint is simply someone who leads a very holy life. But it's only after they die that people find out how "saintly" they were and they become known as Saint Stanislaus or Saint Angela or Saint Margaret or Saint Paul. Every saint started out as a boy or girl and grew into a saintly person. Were you named after a saint? If you were, why don't you try to find a book that will tell you all about your "name saint?" If you were not named after a saint, what saint would you LIKE to be named after?

There are a lot of "patron" saints (or "special friend" saints)—Saint Rose, a special friend of gardeners; Saint Sebastian, patron of soldiers and doctors; Saint Martha, patron of waitresses; Saint Vincent, patron of wine-growers and vinegar-makers; Saint Clare, patron of television; or Saint Joseph of Cupertino, patron of astronauts. There are lots of saints and lots of names. Who's your favorite?

Read My Lips!

Does your mom or one of her friends wear lipstick? Lots of women do. And they may be surprised to learn that people have been wearing lipstick for over 5,000 years!

And YOU may be surprised to learn that beeswax is one of the things used to make lipstick. God sure taught those bees how to make interesting things…beeswax for lipstick and candles and honey for your pancakes!

How Can a Cat Purr*r*r*?

All of the animals in the cat family—from your friendly neighborhood kitty cat to a ferocious jungle lion—make a purring sound when they are happy or sometimes just to say hello. That's because God made the cat so that it can narrow its voice box, which is called a larynx. When the cat breathes, the air flowing in and out of its lungs is disturbed and that makes the purring sound.

God gave YOU a larynx and lungs but made you so that you can talk instead of purr. What will you talk about today? Will you tell a funny story and make someone laugh? Will you say something mean and make someone sad? Will you get angry and shout and make someone mad? What do you think God would like you to do with your voice box today?

Achoo! God Bless You!

Did you know the first vacuum cleaner was invented way back in 1901 but it was waaay too big and clumsy to use easily. Then, in 1908, there was a janitor named James Spangler who had a job sweeping and cleaning away dust but the dust made him sneeze and cough because he had an allergy. He could have complained a lot and kept sneezing but instead, he decided to do something about it. He invented a SMALL vacuum cleaner he could use to clean without stirring up the dust. It worked so well, he showed his invention to a man named William Hoover and they went into business together, making the Hoover vacuum cleaner—and it was soon a bestseller! The Hoover is still a bestseller today—many, many years after it was invented by a janitor!

The next time you have a dusty nose and sneeze, think about Mr. Spangler who could have complained about his problem but instead, found a way to solve it. Don't you bet God would like you to try to handle your problems that way too?!

Don't Be Cross!

You probably know what a cross looks like—a tall straight line with a shorter straight line across it. It's a symbol to remind us that Jesus died on a cross but rose again to new life. But did you know there are several different KINDS of crosses? Since Saint Peter was crucified upside down, Saint Peter's cross is an upside-down cross. Constantine's cross includes a P and an X—the first two letters for Christ in Greek. And there's also an Anchor cross that has a circle at the top for eternity and a crescent shape (like a new moon) at the bottom, which is a symbol of Mary.

When you're riding in a car or a bus or on a bike or a skateboard, wherever you go, look around and see how many different cross shapes you can spot. You might see one on the top of a church or in a window or on the cover of a book or in the shape of the crossbars of a swing set! Every time you see one, just remember that each one is a reminder of how much Jesus loves you! And that should make you happy—instead of cross!

Oooh...

A Faraway Place

Did you ever think you might like to sail far, far away to live on an island? You MIGHT like to live on the island named Tristan da Cunha— or you might not! This is the most remote island on earth where people still live. It's in the South Atlantic Ocean, halfway between South Africa and South America—over a thousand miles away from the nearest land! Only a few hundred people live there (about as many people as the number of students in a small-size school!). If you lived there and decided you wanted a hot dog or some ice cream, you would probably have to get a ship or a helicopter to bring it to you! Maybe that would be fun—and maybe it wouldn't!

Aren't you glad God made a wide wonderful world where there are big cities and small islands and boys and girls who can dream of faraway places and flying in a helicopter or sailing the ocean blue?

Let's Get Nose-y!

Did you know that the nose God gave you can smell about 4,000 different smells? Whew! BUT did you know a dog's nose can help him find his way home? God knew that dogs would sometimes get lost and couldn't talk to ask for directions so he gave them a different kind of sniffer, a nose that would help them follow their "tracks" back home. But God knew YOU would need a nose that could smell cookies baking in the kitchen or popcorn popping at the movies or wood smoke coming from a campfire where you could roast marshmallows! Get nose-y today and look around and notice all the different kinds of noses God gave to people and to OTHER animals! Whose nose do you like best? And what's your favorite smell? Roses…peppermint…oranges…birthday cake???

The Boy Who Couldn't Go to School

Many years ago, there was a little boy who couldn't go to school because his family was so poor, he had to work to make money to help them survive. He wanted to learn though and he managed to teach himself how to read and write. He worked very hard and when he grew up, he traveled the world as a teacher AND a student. He was 33 years old when he finally got a college degree and four years later, he got a master's degree and then he became the second African American to receive a doctorate degree from Harvard University!

This man's name was Carter G. Woodson and he spent the rest of his life researching and writing about the African American experience and became known as the "father of black history."

The boy who couldn't go to school became the man who spent many years as the head of high schools and colleges in America and other countries.

Maybe some days you don't LIKE to go to school but aren't you glad you don't have to work to try to make money to buy food for your family? When you eat lunch today, tell God thanks for the food and also for the chance to go to school and learn about all the interesting people and places in the world. And ask God to bless all those who aren't as lucky as you are!

Sandcastles

Did you ever go to a beach and squish your toes in the sand or build a sandcastle? Or did you ever play in a sandbox? And did you know sand was once used to tell time?

Sand was used in something called an hourglass. Maybe you've even seen one. It's a tall glass container that looks like it has been tied in the middle. The top and the bottom sections are the same size, but there is sand in the top section. And when all the sand sifts through to the bottom section, you know an hour has passed. Then you turn the glass upside down and it starts all over—the sand slowly running through the midde to the bottom section until you know another hour has passed.

You might also have seen a much smaller glass with just enough sand to measure three minutes—which is the amount of time it is supposed to take to boil an egg or for you to brush your teeth!

Do you brush your teeth three minutes every time? Maybe you should, so you can show God you appreciate him giving you teeth to chew popcorn, pork chops, and pizza—because if you were toothless, you couldn't even eat a SAND-WICH?

What Kind of Dog Is That?

If there's a puppy or a grown-up dog living at your house or in your neighborhood, you know what a dog is—but did you know God made ALL KINDS of dogs? There are big Chow dogs and little Chihuahua dogs, and hunting dogs and sheep dogs and bird dogs. And then God also made a dogfish, which is the name for a small shark, and a dogwood tree, which is the name for a small tree that has pink or white flowers.

Of course, God didn't give those NAMES to the different things he made. People did that. What kind of names would YOU give to a dog, a fish, or a tree. Barkie, Swimmy, Leafy? Nooo....you can do better than that!

Fasten Your Seat Belt!

Have you ever fastened your seat belt to take a trip on an airplane? Whether you have or not, you may be surprised to hear that the largest airport on earth is in Saudi Arabia—but the BUSIEST one is Chicago's O'Hare International Airport. It is so busy that on a usual day, there's a plane either taking off or landing about every 37 seconds! And some travelers must get really hungry while they're waiting to board a plane because the restaurants in that airport sell over 9,000 pieces of Chicago-style pizza every day!

Think of all the places you would like to fly if you could take off today—or SOME day. Then plan some things you and your family could do to help SAVE God's beautiful planet Earth so all those places will still be there for you to visit in the future. (Recycle cans, bottles, newspapers, etc....walk or bike instead of ride to save gasoline...pick up litter....what else?)

Dyn-a-Mite!

Did you ever see something being blown up on TV? It was probably blown up with dynamite, a very powerful explosive which was invented by a man named Alfred Nobel. Mr. Nobel owned a plant in Switzerland where they made nitroglycerin, a very DANGEROUS explosive. But when there was an accidental explosion in his plant and his younger brother was killed, Mr. Nobel resolved that he would find a way to make nitro safer to use.

After many failures, he found a way to mix nitroglycerine and a chalky soil and shape it into sticks. They would NOT explode unless you added a blasting cap so they were safer to use. He called these sticks dynamite, a word that comes from a Greek word meaning "power." And dynamite has been used for construction and demolition jobs ever since.

But you know what? Mr. Nobel wanted to be known for something besides the explosive dynamite. He had made a lot of money so when he died, he left money to be given as international prizes to people who had done something to improve the world. The Nobel prizes have been given every year since 1901 to people who have done outstanding work in various fields like chemistry, physics, medicine, literature, and world peace!

Many famous people have won these prizes, including Mother Teresa, a nun who worked in India to help the poor and the dying.

What "field" would you like to work in? What Nobel prize would you like to win—the one for chemistry, physics, medicine, literature, or world peace?

Is There a Boat That Can Float On—and Under—the Water?

You guessed it. It's a submarine. But how can it do that?
Did you know the submarine is built with lots of EMPTY
spaces in it? When it's on top of the water, those spaces are
filled with air. But when the submarine wants to go down, the
crew opens some special doors and seawater flows in and fills
up the spaces—and, since the water is heavier than air—the
submarine sinks under the water.

Would you like to ride in a submarine and travel UNDER
God's ocean? Or would you rather ride in a sailboat on top of
the ocean…or maybe swim IN the ocean? Aren't you glad
God made the oceans and rivers and streams and lakes? Aren't
you glad God made water so you can get a drink when you're
thirsty? Maybe you should tell him thanks.

Keep Pedalling!

A bicycle can be lots of fun but it can't go ANYWHERE without somebody like you. The bicycle will just sit there, alone and useless, until you come along and step on the gas!…or step on the pedals!

You've probably noticed that the pedals are connected to a small wheel with TEETH that is called a gear and the teeth hold a loop of chain that runs between the pedal gear to another gear on the back wheel and when you step on the pedals, the front gear turns and the chain moves and turns the back gear which moves the back wheel…and awaaaay you go.

You probably also know there is a three-wheeled cycle called a tricycle but did you know there is also a ONE-wheeled cycle called a unicycle which is VERY hard to ride? You might see someone riding a unicycle in a circus and maybe some day you might like to try riding a unicycle yourself but TODAY why don't you ask if you can ride your BIcycle to take some cookies or a special treat to a neighbor or friend who is sick or lonely? If you can't, you could say a prayer for that person and then maybe you could just ask if you could eat a cookie while riding your bike and then both you and your bike would be using your "teeth" at the same time!

A Famous Cook Who Was Not a Cook

Did you ever hear of Captain Cook? His name did not mean that he was a good cook but he WAS a great explorer. A long time ago, when there were no airplanes or helicopters or even telephones or automobiles, people only knew what the world looked like in the town where they lived—but some were very curious about what might be out there in the REST of the world. And some of the bravely left home to explore and discover. They had to travel by horse or camel or boat—or walk!

Captain Cook traveled for years, leading explorations to Newfoundland and Labrador, New Zealand and Australia, and was credited with the discovery of Hawaii, which is now the fiftieth state of the United States. People were amazed and delighted when he came back with many stories of different kinds of lands, different kinds of people and plants and foods and customs.

Do you know someone who is a good storyteller? Do you like to listen to stories of adventure? Did you ever hear some of the stories from the Bible? Did you know some of them are even more exciting than Captain Cook's adventures?

Is It a Mite Or a Tite?

Did you ever go way, way down into a hole in the ground called a cave? A lot of people like to explore caves and some are open for tourists to visit with a guide. Caves are dark and maybe a little scary but when you shine a light inside of them, some are beautiful! As you enter a cave, sometimes you have to go through a very narrow place and then you come out into a very large "room." When the guide shines a light in the room, you may see some strange,  long things that look like brownish icicles hanging down from the cave ceiling. These are called STALACTITES.

They were made when water dripped through a crack in the roof very slowly for maybe hundreds of years. There was a mineral in the water called lime carbonate and although the water gradually evaporated (dried up), the mineral from each drop attached itself to the mineral in the next drop until it formed these spiky, strange-shaped stalactites. And then the same thing happened on the floor of the cave so there are upside-down icicles sticking UP from the floor and they are called STALAGMITES. Sometimes the stalagmites grow UP so high, they meet the stalactites coming DOWN and form one big column in the cave.

Would you like to be a cave explorer or would you rather just read about the mites and tites? Either way, isn't it exciting to know that there are mysterious and beautiful things under God's earth as well as on top of it?

What Is Vexillology?

Can you guess what that long word means? Could it mean something about vegetables…or Volkswagens…or VCRs? No. Could it mean something like vexatious—which is the way you feel when you are troubled or irritated (like you might feel when you are trying to program the VCR)? No.

The very long word, vexillology, means the study of FLAGS! It's probably called that because a vexillum was once a flag used by the Romans. Now you know the United States flag is red, white, and blue with stars and stripes, but did you know that every country—and even every state—has a flag with a special design?

In 1959, when Alaska became a new state in the United States, the officials held a contest and invited CHILDREN to design its new flag. A 13-year-old boy won the contest with his design of a blue flag with gold stars forming the Big Dipper and the North Star.

Would YOU like to design a flag for a state or a country? Usually flags have designs with a message—like the 50 stars on the United States flag tell you there are 50 states. What if you were asked to design a flag for God? What designs would you use to tell about God—a heart (for love), a flower or tree (for the things God made), a cross (for Jesus), or maybe a smiley face? How would your flag look?

Does the Secret Service Allow Animals in the White House?

In addition to lots of human animals who have lived in the White House, there have been plenty of dogs and cats—and also some very strange pets. John Quincy Adams had a pet alligator and Calvin Coolidge kept a pygmy hippopotamus! Zachary Taylor let his favorite horse graze on the White House lawn and Warren G. Harding had an Airedale terrier who had his own chair to sit on at Cabinet meetings.

And then there were some pets who had interesting names. President Theodore Roosevelt had a cat who had extra toes on her feet and was called Slipper…President Lyndon Johnson had two beagles named Him and Her…and President Jimmy Carter's daughter, Amy, had a cat with the fancy name of Misty Malarky Ying Yang.

What's your favorite pet or your favorite name for a pet? Don't you think God had a great idea when he made pets so people could have four-legged friends—even in the White House?

Could You Drink Milk From a Milkweed?

No, no, you wouldn't like that at all. This weed has pretty pink flowers and if you break the stem, a white juice comes out that LOOKS like milk—but it isn't. It's called latex and can be used to make rubber so you definitely would NOT want to even taste it. This plant is absolutely NOT eat-able (or drinkable)—but because it provides this juice that looks like milk, somebody named it milkweed.

Who but God would decide to make a milkweed AND a milk cow—a weed with milky juice that can be used to make rubber balls and rubber tires and rubber duckies….and a cow with milk that can be used to make ice cream and whipped cream and milk shakes! God must have known that you would like to play and ride and drink milk and have ice cream treats! Aren't you glad he did?

Time for a Tuxedo!

Did you ever see a picture or a video of the birds called penguins? They LOOK like they are wearing black-and-white tuxedos like the suits men wear at weddings and other very special events—because that's the way God made their feathers. And since they have feathers, do you think they can fly? Sorry, no, they can't.

But guess what? There's another bird that lives in the cold Arctic and looks a lot like the penguin and it CAN fly. And guess what it's name is? It's called an auk! That sounds like what you might say if you swallowed a bug—but of course you would never do that, would you?

If you could make a new kind of bird, what kind would YOU make? What color would it be? Would it fly or walk or jump? Would it talk? Would it be as interesting as some of the birds God made—like a penguin or an auk?

Who Wants to Croodle?

What? You don't know what that word means? Well, most people don't. It means to snuggle, the way a little puppy dog snuggles against the mommy dog or baby chickens creep close under the mother hen…or the way children might squeeze together around a campfire or a fire in the fireplace.

See! You have probably croodled and didn't know it! It's cosy to snuggle on the sofa while someone reads you a book or to snuggle in your bed to say good-night prayers. You DO always say good-night prayers, don't you? Saying a Good Night and Good Morning prayer to God every day is a nice croodly thing to do!

How Could a Leaf Help You Breathe Better?

The little ole leaf has a big job—it's a food factory for its plant. It brings up water from the plant's roots in the ground and it takes in a gas called carbon dioxide from the air. Then, when the sun shines on the leaf, chlorophyll (which is the green coloring in the leaf) uses the energy from the sun to turn the carbon dioxide (which came from the air) and the water (which came from the ground) into food.

After it feeds itself, the plant gives off a gas called oxygen—which is just what humans need to breathe! Now this sounds kind of complicated and the process has a long name—photosynthesis—but that's the way a leaf can help you breathe better. That's why it's nice to have lots of plants in your house and lots of plants in your garden—so the plants can give off oxygen to freshen up the air you breathe! Who but God could think of a way to make a little leaf manufacture something that humans need to breathe and live! (Could you call this a plant giving CPR to a person? Maybe.)

Whew!

Ring, Ring, Ker-Ching! ✳ ✴

D id you ever buy something at a store where they had a cash register that rang up the sale and made a funny noise like KER-CHING? Today cash registers where you buy a hamburger or a T-shirt might be too modern to make that noise but for many years, there was a ker-ching cash register in almost every store.

But did you know that the FIRST cash register was called a "thief catcher"? That's because a store owner named James Ritty wanted to find a way to keep track of sales because some of his employees would slip some money in their pockets instead of putting it all in the cash box. One day Mr. Ritty was on a boat and saw a machine that counted how many times the boat's propellor turned—and this gave him an idea! Why couldn't he invent a machine that would count MONEY and add up how many sales were made. With the help of his brother, he did just that AND he added a bell that would ring each time the "cash drawer" opened. This ker-ching sound turned out to be a good thief catcher and the inventor sold lots of his new cash registers to other business owners and soon the ker-ching was a familiar sound in stores all over the country.

Now if you had a lemonade stand or sold some old toys at a garage sale, you wouldn't need a cash register to ring up your sale—but you COULD make some money that way so you could drop it in the collection basket at church on Sunday. Wouldn't that be a good idea?

Unscramble these letters to see what makes lots of today's modern "cash registers" work. M U R E T P O C

___ ___ ___ ___ ___ ___ ___ ___

COMPUTER

39

A Bowl of Pins in an Alley?

Bowling is a fun game but you don't use a bowl to play it! Instead, you use a big ball and you roll it across the floor to try to knock down some tall things that look kinda like big wooden milk bottles but are called pins—and the 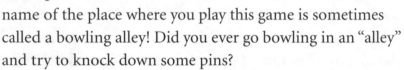 name of the place where you play this game is sometimes called a bowling alley! Did you ever go bowling in an "alley" and try to knock down some pins?

Here's an interesting thing about those "pins." The people who run the bowling alley usually use the same pins for only two weeks and then they let them "rest" and switch to a second set for the next two weeks—and then they switch back. They say the pins get knocked around every day by the bowling balls and wear out fast BUT they will last longer if they use two sets instead of one and let them work for a while and rest for a while!

It's the same way with people. If they work hard all day every day, without any rest, they get all worn down. That's why God told us to "keep holy the Sabbath day"—to work hard for six days but to always save one day in the week to rest and pray and go to church and visit with God and have some fun time with the family. Isn't that a good idea? Does your family save one day a week for "The Lord's Day"—to rest and pray and visit and have fun?

Skating on Thin Ice

Did you know that about one-tenth of the earth's surface is covered in ice? And the coldest place on earth is Antarctica where the record cold is over 100 degrees BELOW zero? Brrr! Would you like to live somewhere that is VERY cold? It's fun to go ice skating or eat ice cream or build a snow fort but some of Antarctica is so cold that the only animal that can live there year-round is a penguin. Brrr!

Now you might think that since Antarctica is so cold, Santa's North Pole would be there. But no…the South Pole is in Antarctica! If you have a world map or one of those big round world globes in your house, why don't you get it out and see if you can find the North Pole and the South Pole? If you don't have one, maybe you could look at one at the library or at a friend's house. You may be surprised at all the names and all the places in God's wonderful world—both the very cold ones AND the very warm ones!

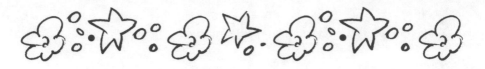

The "Hero" Who Discovered Hot Chocolate!

Would you like to have a nice big cup of hot chocolate right now? Wouldn't that taste good? It's very easy to make today by just adding hot water to a mix…or you can make it with sugar and cocoa and hot milk. But you might never have tasted it if it wasn't for a "heroic" Spanish explorer named Hernando Cortés.

A long, long time ago, in the year 1519, Cortés traveled all the way from Spain to Mexico, and the Aztecs there served him a delicious chocolatey drink he had never tasted before. He found out how to make it and when he went back home to Europe, he told people there how to make cocoa and they told people in America how to make it. But it probably took a long time to cook it back then because you had to use cocoa BEANS instead of the powdery cocoa you use now.

In fact, it was over 300 years later, in 1828, when a chemist named Coenrad Van Houten invented a way to make "powdered" chocolate—and it was much later than that when somebody discovered that hot chocolate tasted even better if you put a marshmallow in it!!!

Bet you didn't know it took so many people and so many years to help you have this creamy chocolate drink. And they couldn't have done it if God hadn't made cocoa beans and sugarcane and cows!

Cold Winter Coats and Cool Summer Ones

Do you wear different clothes in the winter than you do in the summer? Unless you live somewhere where the weather always stays the same, you wouldn't wear a swimsuit in winter or a heavy coat in summer. But did you know some animals change their clothes too? Most kitty cats have heavy fur in the winter to keep them warm but when summer comes, some of their fur falls out so they can be "cool cats."

But God also made some animals who have fur that changes COLOR when the weather changes! The arctic fox, who lives in Greenland, is one. When the snow comes, his fur turns white so he can hide in the snow. God made each of his animals in a special way—just like he made YOU in a special way. Aren't you glad he did?

In the Blink of an Eye

Can you guess how many times you will blink your eyes in your lifetime? No one even thinks about blinking an eye but most people blink their eyes regularly—probably once every two to ten seconds. Some blink faster than others, but just suppose you blink your eyes every five seconds. That would add up to 12 blinks a minute, 720 blinks an hour, and 11,520 blinks a day if you stayed awake 16 hours and slept 8 hours. That's just in ONE day and there are 365 days in a year. So if you live to be 100 years old, you will have blinked your eyes 420 million times! That's a LOT of blinks.

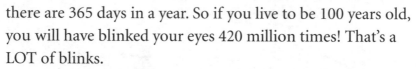

You know God put tears in your eyes and gave you eyelids that can blink so, without even thinking, all day you wash your eyeballs so they won't get dusty. Isn't it great that God gave you built-in eyeball washers—just like your car has windshield washers!

When your car's windshield gets dirty, you have to TURN ON the windshield washers, but God's eyeball washers are automatic!

Oh Beautiful...

Spacious skies…amber waves of grain…purple mountain majesties…the fruited plain. These are all the things Katherine Lee Bates saw when she rode in a horse-drawn wagon to the top of Pikes Peak in 1893. She thought the scene was so wonderful, she wrote a song about what she saw and called it "America the Beautiful." You have probably heard this patriotic song sung on American holidays like maybe the Fourth of July. BUT Katherine Lee was not the first woman to make it to the top of Pikes Peak!

More than thirty years before, in 1858, Julia Archibald Holmes and her husband joined one of the groups of gold-seekers headed for Colorado with the slogan, "Pikes Peak or Bust." Twenty-year-old Julia was a real pioneer who enjoyed the trip, walking beside a wagon, keeping up with the men, and even climbing to the top of the majestic mountain. She wrote to her mother: "In all probability, I am the first woman who has ever stood upon the summit of this mountain and gazed upon this wondrous scene." And she was.

The next time you hear the song "America the Beautiful," think about Katherine Lee Bates and Julia Archibald Holmes and say a prayer of thanks for all the brave women explorers and adventurers who have discovered the beauties of America —and then told the world about them so that others could discover them too!

Bugs for Dinner?

Did you know there's a plant that eats bugs? Yep, it's called the pitcher plant because it has leaves shaped like pitchers. These leaves usually have a liquid inside that attracts insects—and when the bug crawls in to check out the liquid, it gets trapped and "eaten" by the plant. Some pitcher plants will eat any kind of bug that crawls in or falls in the pitcher leaf—the way a family dog will eat any scrap of food that falls on the kitchen floor. But some pitcher plants are picky, picky. They only eat termites!

Bugs and termites probably sound yucky to you but maybe a bowl of cereal or a piece of apple pie would sound

yucky to a pitcher plant! People and plants
and birds and trees and everything on earth
has to "eat" to stay alive—and they all eat
different things in different ways. What is YOUR
favorite thing to eat? Spinach, okra, liver and onions?
Maybe…or maybe NOT. Maybe your favorite might be
cookies, ice cream, hamburgers, or pizza? Whatever it is, be
grateful that you have SOMETHING to eat and always say a
thank-you blessing before your meal. Do you KNOW a
thank-you blessing? If you don't, how about learning this one:

Bless me, Oh Lord,
and bless this good meal;
I thank you, thank you,
from my head to my heel.

OR—if you're saying a thank-you blessing with your family,
you could say:

Bless us, Oh Lord,
and these Thy gifts,
which we are about to receive,
from your bounty,
through Christ, our Lord. Amen.

Who Was Massasoit?

Massasoit was the name of a Native American leader who brought 90 of his men to join the Pilgrims for the first Thanksgiving celebration. The English had decided to have a "harvest feast" to give thanks for all the food they had been able to grow that summer—and were probably surprised when so many Indians showed up to join them. But they were very glad for the opportunity to make friends with the native people—which was not easy since they didn't speak the same language.

This first "Thanksgiving" was not just one dinner on one day in November like Americans have now. Massasoit sent out his men and they brought back five deer and the English had the food they had grown—maybe pumpkins and corn and cranberries—and maybe some wild turkeys. It took awhile to cook all this food so the "feast" lasted at least three days. No one is sure about all the details since there are not a lot of records of those days. The Pilgrims may have invited the Native Americans or Massasoit may have just come over to find out what kind of party his neighbors were having. Either way, it was a very important "happening" since it was a time for making friends and giving thanks—just like Thanksgiving is today.

Would you have liked to be there at that first feast? Do you think they said a "blessing" or some kind of prayer to thank God for the good harvest before they ate? If you had been there, what kind of blessing would YOU have said?

48

A Leaf Is a Leaf—Or Is It?

Did you ever notice a leaf, really notice it? Do you think all leaves are alike? Look again. God made leaves in lots of different shapes—fan-shaped, arrow-shaped, comb-shaped, heart-shaped, and lots more. People notice the bright, pretty flowers, but sometimes they don't notice the leaves that are AROUND those flowers. Start to LOOK at leaves and see how many different shapes of leaves you can find. You might be surprised.

If God took all that trouble to make leaves, just think how much trouble he took to make people in different shapes—tall, short, chubby, skinny, dark, light, with black or brown or yellow or red hair, with blue or green or brown eyes. Just think how much trouble God took to make YOU! That's why he likes you so much and wants you to be his friend.

How Swift Can the Chimney Swift Fly?

Did you know there is a bird called the chimney swift—and it can fly faster than any other bird? It can fly up to 217 miles per hour—and that is an animal speed record. Just imagine—when you are in a car driving fast down a highway, the car is going 70 miles an hour and that seems pretty fast, doesn't it? But this bird can fly more than THREE TIMES faster than that car. AND there is another bird called the frigate bird that can DIVE even faster than the chimney swift can fly. The frigate bird can dive down at almost 250 miles per hour—and that's another animal speed record.

Are you surprised to learn that birds can move that fast? The birds you see in your backyard probably can't fly or dive like that but they ARE fun to watch and nice to have around. If you would like to KEEP them around, you might want to put out a bird feeder and keep it filled with seed OR you might like to make some easy snacks for them. If your mom has some fancy cookie cutters—maybe shaped like a star or a

heart or even just a round shape—there's an easy bird snack you can make.

Lay some bread slices on a cookie sheet or the kitchen counter and use cookie cutters to cut out shapes from the bread. With a pencil, poke a small hole in the top of each shape. Leave the bread shapes laying out all night so they will get hard. The next day, cut some long strips of ribbon or wool thread and string a strip through the hole of each bread shape. Hang the shapes outdoors on the branches of a tree or bush. And while you're hanging these surprise snacks, say a little prayer to thank God for making speedy birds and backyard birds and trees and bushes and whatever else you'd like to add to your thank-you list.

What Is the Softest Metal?

You usually think of metal as being very hard—like the motor of a car or a bulldozer or an iron bar, but can you guess what is the softest metal? It's gold. Now if you've seen a gold ring or a gold coin, it looks pretty hard—and it is—but gold is softer and more bendable than OTHER metals. It is so "soft," it is usually mixed with a small bit of a "harder" metal like copper or nickel before it's shaped into jewelry or coins.

And did you know gold can be melted and it can be beaten until it is only four-thousands of an inch thick (about as thick as a hair!)?

This "soft" metal has always been considered something very special and valuable—so special that gold was one of the gifts the Wise Men brought to the Baby Jesus. If you had a chance to bring a special gift to Jesus, what gift would you choose?

Yippee for the Mississippi!

Have you ever seen a really biiiigggg river? One of them is the great Mississippi River that travels from Minnesota all the way to the Gulf of Mexico. On the way, it flows past Wisconsin, Illinois, Iowa, Kentucky, Missouri, Tennessee, Arkansas, and Louisiana. Now that's a rambling river!

Years ago, when the pioneers were moving west, this river and the "river cities" along the way were very important for the travelers. Remember, there were no airplanes or railroads or buses or even cars, just horses and donkeys and covered wagons—and boats.

Steamboats chugged back and forth, bringing people and supplies to little towns along the way and there were even showboats on the Mississippi. Musicians and actors would live on these boats and the boats would stop at the bigger "river cities." Since people didn't have TVs or even radios back then, it would be an exciting time when they heard the showboat was coming. Everyone would hurry to the riverfront to enjoy the big show. Doesn't that sound like fun?

Now, why do you think God made rivers and lakes and oceans? He could have just made the earth all land—so why do you think he put all those waterways in the world?

The Name Game

Did you know names sometimes have special meanings? According to a "dictionary" of names, Andrew means strong, Justin means fair and just, Patricia means noble, Linda means beautiful, and Dustin means brave fighter. These are all nice names but some REAL people have REALLY funny names. A "name collector" once put together a list of those names and that list included Duckworth Bird, Upson Downs, and Gussie Greengrass!

You could probably look through the telephone book today and make up your own list of real people with really funny names. Or you could use your imagination and make up a list of names you think would be funny.

Do you like YOUR name? Would you like to have a funny name or would you like to have a name that means brave fighter or noble or beautiful or strong or fair and just? If you HAD a name like that, would it describe the way you are or the way you act?

Visiting Aunt Jane

D id you know that you could look at an old map and try to find a country you've heard about—but you couldn't find it because the country changed its name after the map was made? For example, you may have heard about the country of Iran in the news—but Iran was once known as Persia. The country of Thailand was once called Siam and Sri Lanka used to be called Ceylon. So old maps would not have any of those new names and you might think the country you were looking for had disappeared!

One city in New Mexico gave itself a really funny name in 1950. A popular radio show offered to broadcast its anniversary show in any city that would agree to change its name to the name of the radio show. Hot Springs, New Mexico, accepted the offer and changed its name to Truth or Consequences!

So what about Aunt Jane? Well, the popular Mexican city of Tijuana didn't change its name but it DID shorten it. This town was once called El Rancho de Tia Juana—which is Spanish for Aunt Jane's Ranch. So when people visit Tijuana today, they probably don't know it—but they're visiting Aunt Jane!

Would you like to think of a new name for your city or your favorite aunt or maybe for yourself? What new names would you choose? How would you change the names of your friends or any of the places in the world? Sometimes change is hard and sometimes it's exciting. God's world is always changing and YOU are always growing and changing—and sometimes that's hard but it CAN be very exciting to keep changing into a new and better you!

Insect Architects

An architect is someone who designs and/or builds buildings—like schools, churches, grocery stores, and tree houses. So how could an insect be an architect? Well, God made them so they just naturally know how to weave, shape, sculpt, and build! Spiders design and weave very fancy spiderwebs that sometimes look like lace. Wasps make papery nests that have many layers. Termites build houses that are sometimes five feet tall (as tall as some 6th-graders!) and are designed so they have something similar to air conditioning! And bees make wonderful honeycombs full of little round holes they fill with honey. Those are some of the insect architects!

God made other builders too—beavers that build dams, birds that make all kinds of nests and people who build skyscrapers. Would you like to be an architect some day? What would you build? A hospital, an office building, a tree house, a doghouse, a people house? How about a castle or a cathedral?

Who Turned Off the Light?

Sometimes when there's a stormy night, the electricity suddenly goes off—and what do you do then? If you're eating dinner, you can't see where the food is on your plate. If you're reading a bedtime story, you can't see the book! You need light!

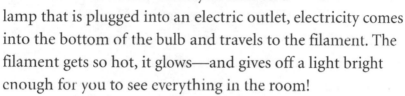

Soon the electricity company fixes the problem and the light bulbs go on again. But how do they do that? Well, inside the glass light bulb, there's a glass tube, a glass rod, some straight wires, and a little coil of wire called a filament. When you turn on a lamp that is plugged into an electric outlet, electricity comes into the bottom of the bulb and travels to the filament. The filament gets so hot, it glows—and gives off a light bright enough for you to see everything in the room!

A lot of people worked to invent electricity but a man named Thomas Edison made the first practical light bulb and later developed the first central electric-light power plant. Aren't you glad God made Mr. Edison so talented and so inventive? But did you know God gave each person a special "talent"? Some people can sing or play music or paint pictures or write books or play ball or be kind to others or be a good housecleaner or automobile mechanic or truck driver or smile and tell funny stories and make other people happy. There are so many "talents," you couldn't even list them all. Which talent do you think God gave you? Ask God to help you find out which is your special talent—and teach you how to use it.

What Are "Noble" Metals?

The word *noble* describes something that is excellent, impressive and has outstanding qualities. Noble metals are all that and they also resist chemical changes so they are known as "chemically inactive—especially toward oxygen." Some of the noble metals are gold, silver, platinum, palladium, ruthenium, rhodium, iridium, osmium, and mercury.

You probably don't see iridium or osmium around your house but you may have seen mercury—in a thermometer or a barometer. Mercury is silvery looking and is sometimes called quicksilver and it's often used in scientific instruments. When you have a cold or the flu, the doctor may take your temperature by putting a thermometer in your mouth. It may be a digital thermometer or it may be a glass tube that has mercury in it and numbers on it—and if you have a fever, the mercury will get warm and rise up the tube to show the number that indicates how high your temperature is—and how sick you are!

For years, the noble mercury has done a noble job of measuring temperatures so doctors will know how to treat someone with a fever. If you ever had a fever, be sure to take all your medicine—even if you don't like the taste of it—so you can get out of bed and go out and have some noble fun!

But today, why don't you say a prayer of thanks for all the noble doctors and nurses who work very hard to help sick people get well.

What Is the Thirstiest Plant?

Plants get thirsty—just like you do—but probably the thirstiest one is the rattan plant…a strong, flexible cane that can be cut and woven to make wickerwork like chair seats and baskets. This plant is a climbing member of the palm family that can grow to six hundred fifty feet—as long as some buildings are tall. And to prove how thirsty it gets, if you cut off a six-foot piece of this plant, about two pints of clear, drinkable water will pour out—water that the plant has sucked up from its roots!

That's even more than YOU suck up when you drink down a giant super-sized soda! The next time you get real thirsty, think about how God made you and the rattan to be very different—but very alike. The rattan knows that to keep fresh and growing, it has to drink enough water. For YOU to keep healthy and growing, you need to drink about eight glasses of water a day—so that's why you get thirsty. Are you surprised to know that you have something in common with a climbing palm plant?

How Dry I Am!

Snap, Crackle, Pop!

The minute you walk into the movie, you can smell it…
mmmm…popcorn! The minute you put a package of it in
the microwave at home, you can hear it start making funny
kerplunk noises…mmmm…popcorn!

But what makes those dried little yellow corn kernels pop?
God put a surprise in each of those tiny kernels—a tiny drop
of water! When you heat the corn, the water turns into
steam and it wants to escape. Now you know steam is
powerful because it is strong enough to run a steam
engine—so the steam blasts its way out and presto!…the little
yellow corn kernel turns into a delicious white cloud and you
have popcorn.

The next time you have popcorn, think about God's
surprise and say a little prayer to thank God for making such
a fun food!

Are You a Pencil Pusher?

People who work in offices and do a lot of "paperwork" are sometimes called pencil pushers. But anyone who uses a pencil could be called that too—and YOU have probably used a pencil.

Years ago, people had to write by dipping the sharp end of a bird feather into ink, but then came the pencil—and then the ink pen and the ballpoint pen and the typewriter and the computer and then e-mail!

But a lot of people still use pencils which are usually round and made of wood with a thin black center section that will make marks on paper when you draw or write. Although these are often called "lead pencils," the "marker" in the center is usually made of something called graphite. In fact, there's a Cumberland Pencil Museum in Keswick, England, where they will tell you how Keswick was the first place in the world to make pencils with graphite.

Would you like to tour a pencil museum? Maybe some day, but not today. Instead, you COULD use today to pick up a pencil or pen and write a note or pick up a crayon and draw a picture and send it to someone who will be happily surprised to hear from you.

Who will that be? Maybe a grandma or grandpa, an aunt, an uncle, a neighbor, or a good friend. Or you could write a little note to God, who would also be happy to hear from you!

Where's the Milky Way?

It COULD be the way to the refrigerator to get a glass of milk to go with your cookies or sandwich or chocolate cake. OR it could be the way to the grocery to buy a candy bar. OR it could be waaay up in the sky where there's a huge white "pathway" of thirty thousand million stars—a sparkly, shining band of light called the Milky Way.

God made the cows that give us milk and the stars that give us shining light at night and the ingredients used to make the candy—but people milk the cows and make the candy and study the stars. God and people working together make a dynamic duo. That's why there's a saying, "There's nothing that God and I can't do—if we work together." What do you think YOU should do—milk cows, make candy, study stars? OR go to school and study to learn all the stuff you'll need to know so you can do lots of OTHER things?

Could a Plant Weigh More Than a Puppy Dog?

Yes, ONE plant could! It has a strange name—the corpse lily—and it grows a strange way too. Instead of growing out of the ground, it grows on the stems or roots of woody tropical forest plants. It can grow to be as round as a birdbath and weigh as much as 18 pounds—which is more than lots of puppies and some small dogs weigh!

You might never come across this kind of lily, but there are lots of other kinds of the lily. You've probably seen the pretty white Easter lily and there's a tiger lily and a Turk's-cap lily and the orange day lily that grows in lots of backyards.

What's your FAVORITE flower? Wasn't it a good idea of God's to make so MANY different kinds of flowers so everybody can have a different favorite!

Nighty-Night

When you play hard or work hard, you get verrrry tired and your body needs to rest. When you get soooo tired, you may not breathe as deep as you usually breathe so your  body goes on alert and tries to make up for that by making you take a big gulp of air all at once. And do you know what happens then? You yawn!

Did you ever yawn when you are sleepy or maybe just when something is booooorrring? It's not polite to yawn when something is boring, but sometimes you just can't help it. It's REALLY not polite to yawn in somebody's face so if you just HAVE TO yawn, you should politely put your hand over your mouth, please.

Whether you're sleepy or bored, isn't it great that God made your body so it keeps check on you and sends a gulp of air to your brain when you forget to breathe deep enough?

If you're bored, maybe you just aren't paying attention but if you're yawning because you're sleepy, it's time to take a nap or go to bed so your body can get the rest it needs. When you're growing, you need LOTS of sleep—at least 8 hours every night—so you can KEEP growing and get up to play hard or work hard tomorrow.

Are you tired and sleepy now? Are you yawning? Well, then…. nighty-night!

The FBI Wants Your Toe Prints

You probably know all about fingerprints. On TV, you might have seen the police taking a criminal's fingerprints—and the FBI keeps a file of fingerprints to use in solving crimes all over the country. It's easy for them to identify anyone by fingerprints because one person's fingerprints are different from every other person's.

But did you know your fingerprints began to form even before you were born—with squiggles and lines and patterns all your own? And did you know your TOE prints and the prints on the bottoms of your feet and the palms of your hands are ALSO different from anybody else's? Yes, you are truly one-of-a-kind!

So wiggle your toes and waggle your fingers, stamp the bottoms of your feet and clap the palms of your hands—and thank God for making you such a special one-of-a-kind!

Going to the Dogs

Did you know that some of the stars in God's sky have been given names—and one of the stars is named Sirius, the DOG Star? This star becomes visible in the Northern Hemisphere in mid July and the ancient Greeks thought this star was SO bright it made the weather extra hot! That's why people started calling the days of July and August the "dog days of summer"!

Do you like really hot summer weather? If you do, here's a Dog Days game to play. Invite some friends over and give each one a blown-up balloon and a spray bottle filled with water. On the count of three, everybody throws his or her balloon in the air and tries to KEEP it in the air by squirting it with water! The one who keeps a balloon up in the air the longest wins the Dog Days prize! (By the way, it might be a good idea to wear swimsuits for this game.)

The Name Game Again

H ere are the meanings of some more names from the "name book"…Susan means graceful, Clarence means famous, Melinda means gentle, Richard means powerful, and Wanda means wanderer. And then there was a man who lived in Philadelphia and his name was Mr. Wolfeschlegelsteinhausenbergerdorff, BUT it wasn't his last name that was so interesting. In addition to that loooong last name, he had 26 FIRST names, one that began with each letter in the alphabet! His names began with Adolph, Blaine, Charles and ended with Xerxes, Yancy, and Zeus!

Do you guess his parents gave him all those names or do you think he maybe got the idea to add that alphabet of names?

How many names do YOU have? Most people just have one first name, one middle name, and one last name—like John Henry Jones—but some add a confirmation name or a nickname and most girls add a new name when they get married, so some people have more names than others. Is one of your names a saint's name? If it isn't , why don't you pick out a saint you like and make that your "secret saint" name?

ALOYSIUS BARTHOLOMEW JONES. BUT YOU CAN CALL ME AL.

Workers on the Wing

All the colorful birds—the red, blue, yellow, etc.—are SO pretty that you might think God made them just to decorate the trees and the sky. They DO decorate the world, but God ALSO gave them another job to do. If you have a garden, some bugs can be good for it but some can destroy it by chewing up flower petals and leaves or sucking sap from stems. And that's when the birds go to work.

Chickadees, wrens, woodpeckers, purple martins, and cardinals are just a few of the birds who gobble up destructive bugs and cutworms and mosquitoes so that your garden can grow and bloom—and so you won't get so many mosquito bites.

If you have work to do today, act like the birds and sing while you work, with a silly little song like this…

In the sky, in the tree,
Birds as pretty as can be…
Workers on the wing,
Singing…Ring-a-ding, ding!

Small Bone, Long Bone, Funny Bone!

Now you know God put lots of bones in your body and they're attached to muscles so they hold you together and help you walk and talk and make a fist and kick a football. But do you know what your smallest and your longest bones are? Well, the smallest bone is in your ear! It's called a stapes and this tiny bone, along with two other bones almost as small, helps you hear. The stapes is also called the stirrup because it is shaped like the stirrups you would put your feet into if you rode a horse.

Going from your head to your leg, the longest and strongest bone is your thighbone, which connects your knee to your hips—and it is called the femur.

None of your bones are really funny since they are very important to help you climb trees and do chores or run errands for your family. But there's a spot on your arm near your elbow that people CALL your funny bone (although it isn't a bone, it's a nerve, and if you hit it, it really hurts). AND if you see something funny—like a dog chasing his tail or a friend making a silly face—and you laugh, then people say that what you saw "tickled your funny bone!"

What kind of silly things tickle YOUR funny bone the most? Do you like to hear funny stories or jokes or riddles or play silly games? Could you tell a funny story or play a silly game today with a friend who's sick or sad? Maybe you could cheer someone up by tickling someone's funny bone!

Which Is Scariest—
Lightning or Thunder?

Lightning LOOKS exciting and even pretty sometimes—but it is very dangerous. Thunder SOUNDS very scary, but it's just loud.

Strange as it may seem, the little raindrops in a cloud have charges of electricity in them. Some of the charges are positive and some are negative. When a group of raindrops with positive charges run into a group with negative charges, they send off a spark or flash of electricity—and that flash across the sky is what we call lightning. The lightning can flash across a cloud or from one cloud to the other or from a cloud to the earth. And that's when it is very dangerous—when lightning strikes something or someone on the ground.

The lightning is very

hot so it can burn a building or kill a person. And since it IS hot, it heats up the air around it as it travels through the sky. That hot air moves so fast it bumps into the colder air around it, and then goes BANG—and that's when you hear a clap of thunder, a noise that gets your attention but can't hurt you.

Do the charged-up raindrops sound like two boys or two girls or two grownups who might run into each other— when one thinks positive about something and the other thinks negative? They might send off sparks too and even get into a fight—and that's when it's dangerous and some-body can get hurt. You would never get mad enough to get into a fight would you? It's always better to try to make friends instead of thunder.

What Is the Magic Number?

Here's a math trick you can try on a grownup—or on anyone who knows how to multiply. Your friend won't know—but you will—that the magic number is 99. Tell him to pick any number from 1 to 100—but DO NOT let him tell you what the number is. Then tell him to multiply the number by 99. Suppose he picks 33. He will multiply that by 99 and get 3,267. Now tell him to add the numbers of his ANSWER. He'll add 3 + 2 + 6 + 7. Now, without knowing what number he picked, you can tell him that the answer is 18. So how did you know that? Because whatever number he picks, the answer will always be 18. Try it and see.

Now you know the magic number is 99. But what is the magic word? It's please. Try it and see!

E-Mail, Snail Mail or Airmail?

Today people send e-mail messages that are delivered very quickly, but back in 1918 letters sometimes took a long time to get from one city to another. So, since the airplane had just become a new kind of travel, the post pffice decided to try using airplanes to move the mail faster.

The first scheduled airmail flight, from Washington, D.C., to New York City, was scheduled for May 15 and a crowd of people, including President Woodrow Wilson, gathered to watch this exciting event. BUT the plane wouldn't start. Finally, the embarrassed pilot realized that the plane's gas tank was empty! Mechanics filled the tank and the plane soared into the sky—but to everyone's surprise, it headed south instead of north. An hour later, the even-more-embarrassed pilot called to say his compass didn't work so he had gone off in the wrong direction—and then the plane had crashed and was upside-down in a cornfield! The post office had to send a car to pick up the pilot AND the three sacks of mail.

Airmail got off to a bad start, but it has worked great ever since.

Did you ever get off to a bad start? Did you ever try to learn something new and just couldn't get it right? Did you ever feel clumsy or stupid or embarrassed because you got something wrong? Well, just ask God to help you and then keep trying—and remember the airmail service. They started off bad but soared to success!

Who's Got the Furcula?

The next time you have a chicken or turkey dinner at your house, instead of asking for the chicken wing or the turkey leg, you might want to ask for the furcula—because that's the wishbone! There's an old superstition that if you get the wishbone (the forked front bone that is shaped like a V), you can choose somebody else to hold one side of the bone while you hold the other side—and then you both make a wish and pull. When the wishbone breaks, whoever holds the biggest half will have their wish come true.

Of course, that's just an old superstition. If you really wish for something, the best way to get it is to pray for it and work for it. If you wish for better grades in school, the only way to get them is to pray for help and then work as hard as you can. If you wish for a pony or your own jet plane to take you to school, well…that may take even more than prayer and hard work!

Have You Got Any Sense?

W ell, of course you do. You have FIVE senses—sight, sound, smell, taste, and touch. You see with your eyes, hear with your ears, smell with your nose, taste with your tongue, and touch with your skin. All of these five "senses" work with your brain to help you figure out what's happening! Some people think that brain of yours is like a computer, but they're wrong. God made your brain much smarter and gave it lots more imagination than a computer. Of course, YOU have to use your senses and log on to your brain to keep it working as well as it should, every day in every way.

Which of your brain "programs" will you call up today…one to help you write or draw or pray or dream? Daydreaming or talking to God or having an adventure by traveling in your imagination—these are things that your computer is definitely not programmed to do.

Pass the Salt

Is there a salt shaker on your kitchen table? Do you ever shake salt on something you're having for dinner? Well, where do you guess that salt came from? Yes, of course it came from the grocery store—but where did it come from before that?

Salt comes from the sea and in some places, there are layers of rock salt where seas dried up years and years ago so salt companies dig it up and break it up and ship it out. They have salt mines to do this just like they have coal mines and diamond mines.

A long time ago, salt was so scarce it was almost as valuable as diamonds! But today, salt is plentiful and it's not just used in kitchens—it's also used in making glass, pottery, textile dyes, soap, etc.

Aren't you glad God put salt in the seas so it can be sprinkled on French fries and popcorn to make them taste so good? They just wouldn't taste the same without that sprinkle of salt! Yum, yum.

Now Where Did I Put That?

Did you ever hide something and then forget where you hid it? When somebody hides something, they sometimes say they "squirreled it away." That's because squirrels are always hiding things. Did you know that in the fall, a squirrel hides as much as 600 quarts of food—saving it for the winter? But then the squirrel does just what YOU do. He forgets where he hid it all!

When spring comes, the squirrel has probably only found 60 of the 600 quarts of food he hid. But a squirrel is not very big so he probably got by just fine with what he found! And besides, squirrels are always so busy, maybe they just like to play hide and seek and don't really care if they forget some of the things they hid!

Do you ever play hide and seek? Do you ever hide when you hear someone calling you to ask you to help with a chore or telling you it's time to go to bed? You wouldn't do that, would you?

HMMM... NOW WHERE DID I PUT THOSE NUTS?

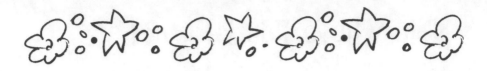

Who's the Shortest of Them All?

After Jefferson, who was one of the tallest presidents of the United States, came James Madison, who was one of the shortest. He was only 5 feet 4 inches tall and at his Inauguration in 1809 (the day he became president) it was hard to see him in the crowd. But no one could miss his wife, Dolly Madison, because she had a big ostrich feather in her hat that waved high above the crowd!

Dolly became a memorable First Lady. She had lots of parties at the White House and often served what was then a brand-new dessert which was called "ice cream." And when the British set fire to the White House, she was the one who saved many of the treasures and got them carried away to a safe place.

But President Madison is even more memorable because he helped create the Constitution of the United States and wrote nine of the first ten amendments which became known as the Bill of Rights.

Do you like to study history and find out all about the things that happened before you were born? So many people did so many heroic things to make the world you live in today. Of course, you don't have to do something special to be a hero…being the GOOD holy, happy person God wants you to be is the most heroic thing anyone can do!

Stick Out Your Tongue

No, no…don't stick out your tongue AT somebody…that's not polite….BUT if you stick out your tongue and look at it in a mirror, you can see that it has little bumps on it. These are called "taste buds" and they let you taste the difference between the salty taste of a potato chip and the sweet taste of a lollipop or the difference between spinach and chocolate ice cream! Your tongue helps you eat by moving the food around so your teeth can chew it…and after you've chewed it carefully, your tongue helps you swallow it.

AND your tongue helps you to talk! Now you know that is very important. Just try saying "I love lollipops" without moving your tongue!

Aren't you glad God made your tongue so you can taste and talk and lick your lips when they get dry? And aren't you glad you have good manners and KNOW that it is NOT polite to stick your tongue out and make an ugly face? Only someone with BAD manners would do that! Right?

Well you're just as pretty as a... a...

Who Said That?

Did you ever hear someone say, "That's sour enough to make a pig squeal!" or "He's up a creek without a paddle!" or "She's as nervous as a long-tailed cat in a room full of rocking chairs." These are silly sentences that we just call "old sayings" because people have been saying them for a long time but we don't know who said them first or why they keep being repeated! Sometimes one family has "old sayings" of their own that another family may have never heard. One grandma might say, "He's as ugly as sin" and another might say, "She's as pretty as a peach."

Are there any old sayings like that in your family? If you can't think of any, why don't you ask your mother or aunt or cousin and see if there are some you haven't heard yet. And then you can giggle and think how nice it is that each family has sayings, customs, traditions, favorite foods, etc., that belong ONLY to that family. And yet there are some things that MOST families say or do or enjoy. So families are different and also alike. That's the way God's whole world is. Wherever you go, you'll find some things that are different and some that are alike!

Take Off That Mask!

Do you know who wears a mask? Well, a raccoon LOOKS like he's wearing a mask, Batman wears a mask, and lots of kids wear masks on Halloween—but there's a different kind of "mask" that people wear sometime to cover up how they feel. A man may be very mad at his boss, but he covers his face with a smile, pretends everything is just fine and keeps working. A lady may be so sad she wants to cry, but she makes her face look happy and everybody thinks she's doing OK. And a boy may be really scared about getting a shot, but he acts real cocky and brave and laughs and kids around so nobody will guess.

You've probably worn a mask on Halloween for fun but did you ever wear a "mask" so nobody would know how you feel? Sometimes that's good…sometimes acting brave or happy helps make you FEEL brave and happy. But when you have a REAL problem, it's probably best to try to take off your mask and talk to somebody about it. And then it's a good idea to tell God about it too.

Riddle-Dee-Dee!

What is gray and has a tail and a trunk? Did you say an elephant? Wrong. It's a mouse going on vacation!

Why does a boy tiptoe past the medicine cabinet? So he won't wake up the sleeping pills!

What is black and white and has sixteen wheels? A zebra wearing roller skates!

There are so maaaany crazy riddles. What's your favorite one? Riddles are silly and fun too. But here's a serious riddle/puzzle: why do people throw cans and bottles and papers and trash all over our nice streets and pretty countrysides? That's a silly thing to do, but it is NOT funny. Tell all your friends that trash belongs in a trash can, NOT in your house or your neighborhood or your city or your world.

Then you can tell them this riddle: What did the elephant do when he tripped on some trash and hurt his toe and couldn't walk? He called a toe truck!

Don't Tip Your Canoe

Do you know which man served the shortest length of time as president of the United States? His name was William Henry Harrison, but his nickname was "Old Tippecanoe" because he had been a hero at a battle at Tippecanoe Creek in Indiana in the year 1811. Several years later, when he ran for president, along with John Tyler who was the candidate for vice-president, they decided to use the slogan, "Tippecanoe and Tyler too!" It must have been a good slogan because they got elected.

But when Inauguration Day came, even though it was very cold and stormy, President Harrison decided not to wear a warm coat or a hat. He rode on horseback in the big parade which lasted for two hours and then gave a very long speech out in the open air. And do you know what happened? He caught a cold. Instead of getting well, he got sicker and sicker and only a month later, he died. Instead of the four years he expected to be president, he was only the president for 32 days so no one ever knew if Tippecanoe would have been a good president.

When it's cold and stormy, do you ever go out without a hat or a warm coat? Even if you're not going to be riding horseback in a parade or making a long speech, you probably should listen when someone tells you to "bundle up because it's cold outside." We have a lot better medicine today than they had when President Harrison got sick, but it's still no fun to be coughing and sneezing instead of playing or building a snowman.

My, How He Grew!

Did you know that a kangaroo can grow up to weigh at least 120 times what he weighed when he was born? Kangaroos are VERY small when they are born but grow up to be REALLY big. This will give you an idea of how they grow—if a new little baby boy that weighs about seven pounds today would grow like a kangaroo does, he would grow up to be an 840-pound man! Can you imagine that!

The kangaroo has very strong back legs for leaping and fighting and short front legs for grabbing and hugging. You probably know that the baby kangaroos live in a pouch on the mama kangaroo's stomach that is like a backpack on her front! And a kangaroo can run about 30 miles an hour. So it's a very INTERESTING animal.

Have you ever seen a real kangaroo? Would you like to travel to Australia where they have lots of kangaroos? It's a very INTER-ESTING coun-try—but then all God's animals and all God's countries are very interesting!

What's in a Name?

Some animals and plants and bugs have names that really fit them—but others don't. A grasshopper is a bug that hops across the grass and a housefly is a pest that flies around your house—so those names fit. But a dragonfly sounds like a huge fire-breathing creature that can fly—and you know it's really a small brightly colored insect with wings that look lacy and fragile. And a peacock sounds like a rooster covered with the kind of green peas you eat for dinner! So the dragonfly and peacock don't exactly have names that fit.

Did you ever know someone who had a name that just didn't fit? Maybe a big tall strong football player that everybody called Junior? Or maybe a delicate little lady that was named Murgatroid? Who do you know with a name that fits just right?

Actually, it doesn't matter what your legal name is. When someone acts good and honorable, people say they "have made a good name for themselves"—and that's what counts.

Pen Names and Nicknames

Did you ever hear of a famous author named Mark Twain? He wrote stories about boys named Tom Sawyer and Huckleberry Finn. But the author's REAL name was Samuel Clemens. Mark Twain was his "pen name," the name he used when he wrote books. And you might not recognize the name Theodor Geisel but that was the REAL name of the man who wrote about *Horton the Elephant* and *The Grinch Who Stole Christmas* so you probably know him by his "pen name," which was Dr. Seuss.

Only authors have pen names but lots of people have nicknames—even criminals. Did you know the FBI has a list of over 150,000 nicknames of criminals? Some of them are Gold Tooth Frenchy, Iron Foot Florence, Clothesline Slim, Fire Alarm Brown, and Step Ladder Lewis (a crook who carried a ladder with him so he could break into second-floor windows!). Criminals also sometimes use aliases—regular-sounding names like Jack Smith or Mary Brown but names that are not their REAL names. If they do that, the police record will include an AKA for "Also Known As," like AKA Alexander Flintnoogle, AKA Jack Smith.

Even God has some AKAs.....he's also called Lord, Jesus, Father, Savior, Christ, etc. And he would like for you to USE one of his names by saying a prayer at least once a day. Will you do that?

Having a Bad Hair Day?

Some hair is curly, some hair is straight, some hair sticks out all funny, and some hair looks great!

BUT whether you're having a bad-hair day or not, did you know your hair helps protect your head? And it helps to keep you warm in winter and cool in summer. And then, going on down your face, you have those hairy eyebrows that help cut down the glare of the sun in your eyes and those eyelashes that are like little window screens so if dust or anything else is flying in the air, it won't come flying into your eyes.

So whether you wish your hair was curlier or straighter, whether you wish you had more of it or would like to shave your head, be glad that God put all those things on your head to protect you. And the next time you raise your eyebrows or flutter your eyelashes or comb your hair, say thanks.

Time for a Change

Did you ever watch a frog jumping around your yard or on the edge of a lake? Did you know that frog began as a tiny little tadpole that lived in the water and had gills so it could breathe in water like other fish do? Then the tadpole grew some back legs and then some front legs and then its tail dropped off and its gills changed into air-breathing lungs and out of the water, hopped Mr. Puddlejumper Frog.

There are a lot of different kinds of frogs—like bull frogs, leopard frogs, and the red-eyed tree frog. Although most frogs live in or near water, some live in tropical forests or even deserts.

The frog changed from a wiggly little tadpole in the water to a champion hopper, leaper, and jumper who could even live in a tree! So did you ever think about how YOU changed too? You began life as a tiny baby who couldn't walk or talk or ride a bicycle or eat a hamburger. And then you grew and changed! Now you have teeth so you can chomp on a pizza and you have learned to talk and sing and read books and play games and your legs have grown so you can hop and leap and jump even higher than the frog! And God made you so that you'll KEEP changing and growing and learning so you can do even more things! Whee!

Did You Ever Meet Mother Goose?

Did you ever hear any stories or rhymes about Old King Cole, Little Jack Horner, Hey Diddle, Diddle, the Cat and the Fiddle, the Cow Jumped Over the Moon? Those all came from a Mother Goose book. And do you know who Mother Goose was?

No, she was NOT a goose who could write. She was a real lady named Elizabeth Foster who married a man named Isaac Goose and became Mrs. Goose. When she had grandchildren, Mother Goose made up stories for them and the stories and rhymes were published in a book and Mother Goose has been a favorite of children ever since!

How many Mother Goose stories have you heard? Humpty Dumpty, Jack Be Nimble, The Three Little Kittens Who Lost Their Mittens? Do you ever like to make up rhymes or poems or prayers? You might make up a silly one like this: Thank you, God, for birds and trees. And tell me, God, do bees have knees?

Why don't you try to make up some poem-prayers right now?

Did You Ever Have Goose Bumps?

When you get really cold, your brain sends a message to some tiny muscles under your skin and those muscles pull up the tiny hairs on your skin and your skin looks bumpy—kinda like a goose's skin. So when you get cold, sometimes you get "goose bumps." Then your brain tells some other muscles to start jiggling around and you start shivering. All that jiggling and shivering sends off some heat and helps you warm up a bit. But goose bumps and shivering don't work as well as a wooly coat and hat and scarf—OR a cup of hot chocolate!

God probably taught your body to give you goose bumps and shivers to REMIND you that when you get sooo cold, it's time to find some place warm or find something warm to drink. Did you ever get goose bumps? Did you take God's reminder and head for home?

How Fast Can You Run?

You are probably a very fast runner, but do you know that animals can run faster than people? The very fastest runner is surely the cheetah. This member of the cat family can run about 70 miles an hour—and some have set a speed record of 75 miles an hour. If a cheetah ran that fast down a highway, he might get a speeding ticket because he would be running over the speed limit!

These sleek, elegant cats were once owned by royalty and aristocrats who liked to watch them run and sometimes used them for sport to hunt down other animals. The emperor Akbar, who ruled India in the sixteenth century, is said to have owned 9,000 cheetahs in his lifetime! These Asiatic cheetahs are very rare today but there are still many African cheetahs who like to chase gazelles who are very fast too and can run about 60 miles per hour. The cheetah's speed record is for sprinting. Within a few seconds, it can reach 70 mph, using its claws like spiked shoes, but it can't maintain a speed quite that fast for long chases.

God made some other animals that can run fast too: an ostrich, 50 mph; a rabbit, 45 mph; an elephant, 24 mph; and a kangaroo, 18 mph.

It's good to run fast when you're in a race but, when you're taking a test, NEVER be a cheetah!

A Theodore Bear!

Did you know that the teddy bear was named after the twenty-fifth president of the United States, Theodore (Teddy) Roosevelt, because he once stopped someone from shooting a baby bear? This president was a sickly child, but he exercised and built himself up enough to become a boxer and then worked as a cowboy and then got the nickname of "Rough Rider" when he led a band of volunteer soldiers called the Rough Riders in a charge up a hill in Cuba and became a hero!

When "Teddy" moved his family into the White House, he had six children who were as energetic as their father. Since they were the "First Family," everything they did made news so people were soon reading in the newspaper about the Roosevelt children's adventures. They walked on stilts over the White House floors, slid down bannisters, and took their pony upstairs in the White House elevator! Maybe they needed some teddy bears so they could have some quiet playtime!

Do you ever have "quiet" time? Do you ever sit under a tree and read a book or sit in the sun and close your eyes and travel to faraway places in your imagination or lay in the grass and watch cloud pictures and tell God stories about what you've been doing or what you'd like to do some day? Try it! You may be surprised to discover what a special, private, happy time "quiet time" can be!

Hi, I'm Teddy Bear!

Painting People

Did you ever watch someone painting a room or a house? Did you ever dye Easter eggs or use watercolors to paint pictures? Then you know that paint comes in all kinds of different colors and sometimes you can mix a bit of two or three colors to get a different color.

The thing that gives the paint its color is called pigment. And guess what…your skin has pigments too! So that's why people's skins can come in all kinds of different colors.

There's a dark pigment called melanin that gives skin most of its color. The more melanin there is, the darker the skin is. There's also a yellow pigment called carotene that adds a different tint to skin. AND the thickness of your skin can affect the color. If you have thin skin, the reddish color of blood under your skin can show through a bit and give you pinker cheeks.

So that's why people come in lots of colors…vanilla, chocolate, cocoa, peach, oatmeal, etc. And all the colors are beautiful.

If the sky and the grass and all the flowers were just ONE color, the world would look pretty boring, wouldn't it? The same is true of people. So aren't we lucky that God painted us a multicolored, many-splendored world?

Who Invented the Alphabet?

Ab, c, d, e, f, g…do you know your ABCs? Sure you do but do you know where they came from? The very first kind of writing was just pictures and then there were symbols and finally letters.

The first alphabet was invented by the Phoenicians about 1,500 years before Jesus lived on earth. The Greeks learned it from them and taught it to the Etruscans and they gave it to the Romans. The Romans made a Latin alphabet about the year 100 and that's the one we use today.

But did you know the name alphabet came from the first two words in the Greek alphabet, which are *alpha* and *beta*? And did you know there are OTHER alphabets used today that are different from the ABC one you use? There is still the Greek alphabet plus Chinese, Russian, Arabic, and Hebrew alphabets. And some use symbols instead of letters.

If you want to send a message to someone, you NEED an alphabet because letters make words and words make sentences and sentences will make a message. But you don't need any of those things to send a message to God. You don't need paper or pencil or postage stamps or a mailbox. You can just think what you want to say to God and he will get the message.

Earley Does It!

Did you ever hear of a lady named Charity Adams Earley? She was the commander of the only all-black Women's Army Corp unit to serve overseas during World War II and the Smithsonian Institution has included her in its listing of the "historically most important black women"!

It took faith and hope for Charity to join up to help fight the war in 1942 after she had graduated from Wilberforce University and was still studying for a master's degree at Ohio State. At that time, the military was segregated and she suffered many humiliations as one of the "colored girls." But she was quickly promoted and by 1945 had risen to the rank of major when she was sent to England to be the battalion commander of a unit which routed mail to millions of members of the armed forces in Europe. (Much of the mail had backed up in English warehouses in the chaos that followed the Battle of the Bulge and mail from home was very important for troop morale!) Because of this, in 1996, Charity was honored at the Smithsonian Institute's National Postal Museum for her wartime service.

With faith and hope (and hard work), Charity reached the high military rank of lieutenant colonel by the time she left the service—and became a "historically important" person.

Of all the people in God's wide world, there are only a few who are historically important, but there are many who have faith, hope, and charity—three important "virtues"? Did you know that these virtues can mean believing in God, hoping for his help, and doing his work by helping others? Having virtue can also mean the "habit" of always trying to do the right thing, the good thing. Do you have that habit?

Zoom! Zoom!

D id you ever watch an automobile race on TV? Some of those cars go as fast as 200 miles per hour! But, way back in 1901, when only a few people had even SEEN an automobile, Henry Ford won a car race with an average speed of 45 miles per hour! He was even behind in the race for seven laps until the car ahead of him lost power and Mr. Ford's car raced ahead to win. His prize was a crystal punch bowl and $1,000.

Today automobile race winners get thousands and thousands of dollars, but Henry Ford was very happy with his prize. Because of winning, he got a lot of publicity and some rich investors heard about the race and gave him enough money to help start the Ford Motor Company.

Up until then, cars had been made one at a time so they were too expensive for the average person. Ford made the first cheap, reliable car by using an assembly line. He sold over 15 million of these Model-T cars and his company became a huge success.

Will you be glad when you are old enough to drive a car and go zoom, zoom down the highway? Do you like riding in a car that's going zoom, zoom down the highway? Don't forget to always keep your seat belt fastened and remind the driver to keep the speed limit. That's the law and God would want you to obey the law.

Oh, and since you know what zoom, zoom is, do you know what oom, oom is? That's a cow going down the highway backwards.

And where is the cow going? To the moo-vies, of course.

Just a Bite!

Did you know you have some teeth with some very strange names? In the front of your mouth, God put incisors. They are sharp so you can bite off things like corn on the cob. In the back of your mouth, he put big flat teeth called molars that are good for grinding things like peanuts. And in between, he put other teeth called canines and bicuspids. But the good thing is that you don't have to even THINK about which tooth to use for which food. Once you learn to eat, your teeth just know how to work together—whether you're chewing on a pizza or a potato.

God had a great design when he made those teeth for you so don't mess up his design. Always remember to brush—AND floss!

What Is a Ha-Ha?

Oh, you say it's a laugh, a chuckle, a giggle, a tee-hee? Yes, but what else? You say it's a snigger, a snickle, a titter, a guffaw? Yes, but what else? You say it's a fence? A fence? Yes, there IS a kind of fence that is called a ha-ha.

At English estates or maybe castles, where there were beautiful gardens and huge acres of lawn, there were also cows and sheep that would wander about unless they were fenced in. But fences did not look nice on those beautiful lawns so instead, the landscapers built grassy slopes of earth. From the castle side they looked like a natural part of the garden, but from the cow's side they were steeply sloped so the cows couldn't climb up them and get in the garden to mess up the view.

And what did they call such a grassy "hidden fence"? They called it a Ha-Ha….like maybe saying "OK cows, so now you can't get in…HA-HA!"

Did you ever hide something so that no one else could see where it was…and then think, Ha-Ha? Maybe that's what God did when he hid pictures in the clouds and made tiny wildflowers that you couldn't see unless you looked very carefully and colorful fish under the water that you could only find if you learned to snorkel. God made lots of HA-HAs in his world, just waiting for you to discover them! So always be on the lookout and then every time you find one, YOU can say HA-HA!

HA HA HA HA HA HA HA HA

A World of Relatives!

When Abraham Lincoln was elected president of the United States in 1861, the vice president that was elected with him was named Hannibal Hamlin. Hamlin served as vice-president until 1865 when Andrew Johnson became Lincoln's next vice-president. It must have been interesting to be vice-president during the Civil War—but there was another interesting thing about Mr. Hamlin. He was one of five children and the other children in his family were named Asia, Africa, America, and Europe! He had a world of relatives!

Do you guess the Hamlins spent a lot of time traveling around America, Europe, Asia, and Africa—checking out the places they were named after? Would YOU like to travel around a lot, visiting faraway—or nearby—places? Would you like to explore the jungles of Africa, visit the Great Wall of China in Asia, travel down the highways and byways in America and Europe? It's fun to discover all the very different parts of God's wonderful world—but it's always nice to come home again. There's no place like home.

 Foxy Loxy

You have probably heard that a fox is sly, but did you know a fox is also shy? Although it's a member of the dog family, the fox is not friendly like a puppy dog so it lives in holes it digs in the ground and you seldom see one because it usually only comes out at night to look for food. The red fox has pointed ears that can hear REALLY good and strong feet and legs. It doesn't run fast, but it can run for long distances at the same speed. And God gave the fox a big bushy tail so when it gets cold, it can curl up and wrap that tail around its body just like a scarf! Isn't that a foxy way to keep warm?

And there's another funny thing the fox does—funny but sly too. Have you ever seen a dog chase its tail, running around and around in circles? Well, sometimes a fox does that—but not for fun. The fox eats small animals so when a hungry fox spots one, he will sometimes start chasing his tail and the small animal will stop to watch him, wondering what that old fox is doing. What the small animal doesn't notice is that that old fox is circling closer and closer, until it's close enough to reach out and grab its dinner!

That's a sneaky thing to do but shy foxes don't get fed by families like puppy dogs do so they have to be sly to get some supper. Do you and your friends ever like to turn around and around until you get so dizzy you fall down and start giggling? Do you ever pull a sly trick on someone or wrap up in a scarf to keep warm? Well, maybe you're a little foxy too!

Shhh...It's a Secret...

When someone tells you a secret and tells you to NOT tell it to anyone else, they might ask you to "zip your lips." They want you to pretend there's a zipper on your mouth so you can't open it! You will also want to zip your lips when you're swimming so you won't swallow any water. And then there are times when you want to OPEN your lips so you can eat or drink or talk. But what else can you do with your lips besides open and close them?

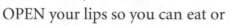

You can pucker your lips to whistle…you can blow through them to blow out birthday candles…and you can use them to breathe in and say "Wheee" when you're happy or to blow out and say "Whew" when you're really tired. Oh, oh, there's one other very important thing you can do with your lips. You can use them to kiss somebody hello or good-bye or good-night. Aren't you glad God gave you lips?

What will you do with yours today—whistle to call your puppy or to whistle a happy tune….whisper to tell someone a secret or to whisper a prayer to God to thank him for your pucker-uppers?

Scrambled Animals

Is a hedgehog a pig that lives in a bush? Is a dormouse a mouse that lives behind a door? Nooo…a hedgehog is a little animal that has both hair and spines and when it gets scared, it rolls itself up into a ball with the spines sticking out. It's also called a porcupine.

A dormouse is an in-between—it looks and acts like either a large mouse or a small squirrel. It lives in bushes or trees and likes nuts and acorns. It usually only comes out at night and hibernates in the winter.

There are also some other creatures who are NOT what they sound like. The bald eagle is not bald but has white feathers on his head so he looks bald at a distance. The sea horse is NOT a horse but a fish. Butterflies are not flying butterballs and houseflies are not flying houses.

Can you think of other things that are not what they sound like? How about a bulldog or a bullfrog? How about a holy terror? That's what people call someone who misbehaves. How can you be holy when you are misbehaving? Which are you—holy or a terror?

Once in a Blue Moon

Did you ever hear of a BLUE moon? Did you ever hear someone say, "That only happens once in a blue moon." Well, there IS something called a blue moon but it only happens once in a VERY, VERY long time.

When you look up in the sky and you see just a crescent-shaped sliver of a moon, that's called a New Moon. Then each night, that sliver gets a bit larger until it is finally a big round circle and you call that a Full Moon. Now it takes a little less than a month for the moon to revolve around the earth so you only see one FULL moon each month or three full moons in each season—summer, winter, spring, and fall. BUT once in a very, very long time, there will be four full moons in one season—and the third one is called a blue moon!

So you can say that it's only once in a blue moon when someone wins a million dollars…or once in a blue moon that someone gets a chance to go on the space shuttle to the moon…or maybe once in a blue moon that you get the kind of lunch you like!

Isn't it amazing how God made the moon and the sun and the stars and the earth and figured out how to make them all revolve without crashing into one another? Amazing!

Did You Ever Make a Cake?

If you've ever helped with the baking or watched someone making a cake, you know you have to put in lots of ingredients and you have to measure them very carefully and be sure the oven isn't too hot or too cold. And believe it or not, that's the same way plastics are made! Several ingredients are measured and mixed and baked and "iced."

The first plastic—celluloid—was invented back in 1870 but since then, the "recipe" has been changed in so many ways that today everything from automobile parts to squeezable mustard jars to toys are made from plastic. And you can even "ice" them with plastic-based paint! Some plastics are hard enough to stop a bullet and some are as soft as cotton balls and can be used in pillows or mattresses. If you try to count all the things in your house or school or playground that are made of plastic, you might not be able to count that high!

And then, think about how God made YOU the same way—mixing together an armful of strength, a handful of talent, a brainful of ideas, a heartful of courage—and an icing of laughter. The good thing though is that you are NOT plastic. You are the real thing!

The "Poet of His People"

Over a hundred years ago, there was a young man named Paul Laurence Dunbar who became known as the "Poet of his People" because of his genius in writing poetry in African American dialect. His poetry helped others understand how slaves felt before and after they were freed.

His first book of poetry was titled "Oak and Ivy" and was published in 1892, when he was working as an elevator operator. And he sold copies of his book for $1.00 each to the elevator passengers. (Did you know that back then, they didn't have the kind of elevators where you just step in and press a button for the floor you want? Every elevator had a "driver" who would open and close the doors and operate the elevator so it would stop at the right floors.)

Even though his health was bad and he died when he was only 33 years old, Dunbar wrote many short stories and novels in addition to his poetry—and became one of many African American heroes.

Did you ever ride in one of those glass-walled elevators where you can look out and see where you're going? Some of them are even on the side of a building so you almost feel like you're flying. Maybe we could make up a poem about an outside elevator:

> Up, up, faster and faster we go,
> Where I WAS is now far below.
> Heading for a cloud is now where I'M
> But whew, we stopped just in time.

Well, maybe you could make a better poem…and a prayer to tell God thanks for heroes like Mr. Dunbar.

King George of the United States?

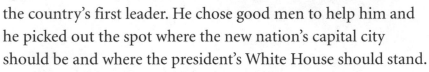

You may have heard of King George of England, but did you know that some people wanted to make George Washington his country's first king instead of its first president? He had always been a leader and was a great general in the Revolutionary War that freed America from England's rule so everyone agreed that he should serve as the country's first leader. He chose good men to help him and he picked out the spot where the new nation's capital city should be and where the president's White House should stand.

But George Washington also liked to fish and hunt and try planting different kinds of crops on his farm—like alfalfa and pecan trees. So after he served two terms as president, he retired and went back to his farm where he enjoyed horseback riding, horse racing, and parties with lots of dancing. But his wife, Martha, saw to it that the parties always ended by nine o'clock—because that was President Washington's bedtime!

What time is YOUR bedtime? Do you always go to bed by nine o'clock? Maybe you should. That would give you plenty of time to say good-night prayers and then dream dreams of what you will do some day…fish, hunt, ride horseback, have parties for your friends, or maybe become a general or a president?

Is There a Magnet in Your House?

If somebody in your house collects refrigerator magnets, there may be LOTS of magnets in your house! But if you have ANY kind of bar magnet, it can be fun to find out WHAT it will attract. Take your magnet around the house and see where it will stick. It will probably stick to paper clips and coat hangers…it might NOT stick to a cooking pot but it might stick to a toaster. You can put a paper clip on top of a piece of paper and the magnet UNDER the paper and if you move the magnet around, the paper clip will move too—like magic. You can even put the paper clip in a glass or in a glass of water and the magnet will still pull it around.

But did you know some people are magnets too? Or at least, it seems like it, because some people are so nice or so much fun, they just seem to draw other people to them like a magnet draws the paper clip! You might say they have a magnetic personality. Do you know anyone like that? If you would like to BE like that, remember the Be-attitudes—be good, be kind, be thoughtful, be helpful, be a friend, be yourself. What could be more magnetic than that!

What a Magnetic Personality.

A Crowd of Clouds

When you look up in the sky and see those clouds floating by, you probably notice that they are all different because they keep changing as they drift past. If you see a cloud you like, you have to look fast before it changes into a different shape. But did you know there are names for certain TYPES of clouds?

The fluffy, puffy, cottony clouds are called CUMULUS which means "mass or heap." The high feathery clouds that kinda look like a horse's tail are named CIRRUS, the Latin name for "lock of hair." Then there are the layered clouds called STRATUS and the high clouds called ALTO and the dark rain clouds called NIMBUS.

There are some combinations of names too, like Stratocumulus and Altostratus and Stratocumulus...but that's probably more than you ever wanted to know about cloud names.

Since these names are so fancy, why don't you make up some better cloud names? What would YOU call the fluffy ones, the feathery ones, or the dark stormy-looking ones? Maybe some day you'll be on TV announcing the weather and you can tell everyone what the really GOOD names are for God's clouds!

Zip, Zip, Stick Tight

Did you know that about a hundred years ago, people had to fasten all their clothes with buttons or laces or maybe safety pins?! Then, in 1913, a Swedish engineer patented a new kind of clasp that would lock and unlock. The Navy tested it on some flying suits and it worked. Then the B. F. Goodrich Company used it on some rubber boots and it worked. It was much faster than buttons or laces because it zipped up and down—so they called it the zipper.

And then, in 1948, another Swedish engineer went on a hunting trip in the mountains and came back with little seedpods called burrs stuck all over his clothes. When he pulled off the burrs, he saw they looked like tiny hooks and they had hooked on to the thread loops of his jacket. After a lot of experimenting, he invented a tape with little hooks that would stick to a tape with little loops. You could press the two together and they would stick and then you could rrrripppp them apart. And you could use the tape over and over again. And he called his new idea Velcro (and got a registered trademark for it). So today lots of jackets and shoes get closed with zippers or Velcro!

Aren't you glad that God gives people such good ideas? Aren't you even gladder that those people don't just THINK about the ideas but they get busy and ACT on the ideas! Does God ever give you a good idea—like maybe you should turn down the loud music so it wont bother your dad or maybe you should do your homework BEFORE bedtime? Do you just think about it or do you DO it?

Mountains of Jewels

There are lots of famous mountains in God's wide world—the Rockies, the Alps, the Appalachians, the Himalayas. And there's the giant Mount Everest that so many people have tried to climb. But did you know there are two mountains named for JEWELS that are both in the same state? The Diamond Mountains and the Ruby Mountains are both in Nevada.

Did you know that it isn't just mountains that are named after jewels? There's the famous Diamond Head, a great high craggy rock jutting out of the ocean in Hawaii…and of course, there's the Emerald City in the Wizard of Oz! Some girls even have "jewel" names like Pearl, Beryl, Ruby, or Opal.

A jewel or gem might be described as precious, treasured, or very dear—but did you know some people are also described as precious, treasured, and very dear? What is your favorite jewel and who is your favorite "jewel" person?

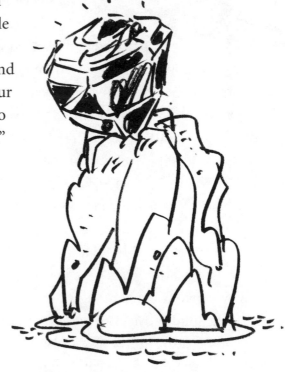

Whoooo Said That?

Someone once started the rumor that you could make an owl wring its own neck if you kept walking around the owl in circles because the owl would keep turning its head to watch you—but that's not true. The owl DOES have very large eyes and when it is watching something, it CAN turn its head upside down and NEARLY all the way around…but NOT all the way around. When its head gets ALMOST all the way around, the owl simply whirls its head rapidly in the other direction and keeps watching.

The wise old owl usually waits until night to come out so it NEEDS those big eyes to see in the dark. And it has fringed "flight feathers" so its flight is silent and you wouldn't hear it coming in for a landing like you would hear an airplane. But do you know what an owl does in the daytime? When the sun comes up, the owl finds a hole in a tree or a spot on a leafy branch and goes to sleep. That's why they call people who stay up very late at night and then sleep very late in the day "night owls."

God made the night dark and mysterious and secret, a time to rest and dream. God made the day bright and busy, light and just right for work or play, a time to go places and do things and maybe daydream. So whether you're a "night owl" or an "early bird," God made both day and night for you to enjoy.

Oops!

Did you ever spill something and make a big stain on a tablecloth? Well, did you know there was a Swiss chemist named Jacques Brandenberger who was TRYING to make a stainproof tablecloth when he ACCIDENTALLY discovered how to make cellophane!

But do you know what cellophane is? It's that clear, see-through, shiny paper that you usually see wrapped around Easter baskets! Cellophane looks very pretty wrapped around any kind of gift basket. And sometimes it's wrapped around lollipops too. And it is NOT named after the cello, which is a musical instrument, but it IS named after cellulose, which is a plant fiber Mr. Brandenberger was using to try to make that stainproof tablecloth.

So now you can enjoy a pretty Easter basket, but you STILL have to be careful not to spill anything on the table-cloth! And sometimes when you do something bad or mean, you might feel like you've "stained" your reputation—which is even worse than staining a tablecloth—but if you tell God you're sorry, he will help you get stainfree again.

Does Your Family Have a Secret Code?

Did you know you and your family DO have a code but it is not a secret—it's your zip code! And the post office gave it to you. Every time you write a letter to anybody or anybody writes a letter to you, they have to put your name, address, AND zip code on the envelope or it won't get delivered.

AND did you know every state in the United States has a two-letter postal abbreviation, which is a short way of writing the state's name? For example, California is a long name but its abbreviation is CA…and Colorado is CO and Florida is FL and Nebraska is NE and Indiana is IN and Washington is WA and Maine is ME and Kentucky is KY and Arizona is AR and Oklahoma is OK and Connecticut is CT.

Another "code" name you might have is Christian (which means you believe in Jesus Christ) or kind (which means you like to help others) or obedient (which means you try to do what your parents or teachers tell you to do).

If you would like to play a game today, why don't you try to make words out of the state abbreviations—add Colorado to Oklahoma and you get cook!…add Colorado to Indiana and you get coin! See how many more you can make.

SSSH

The Sherlock Holmes Seal

The harbor seal is a kinda cute critter because it has the snout of a dog and the long whiskers of a cat—AND, like the famous detective Sherlock Holmes, it's very good at tracking down things. Of course, the seal is not tracking down a criminial—through the murkey, dark waters where it lives, it's tracking down its dinner!

Those seal whiskers are VERY sensitive and can detect very small movements in the water, like the wake (or track) left by a moving fish. When some scientists decided to try to prove how those whiskers worked, they put a blindfold and noise-blocking headphones on a seal! Then they put a miniature submarine in the water and sent it along to see if the seal could follow the submarine's wake. Even with the blindfold and headphones, the seal could follow it at least 80 percent of the time. THEN they put a stocking over the seal's snout, covering up the whiskers and guess what…the seal couldn't track anymore! This proved that it was using its whiskers as a "motion detector" to search for dinner.

Aren't God's animals-AND scientists—amazing! Imagine putting a blindfold or a stocking on a seal!

Why don't YOU put a blindfold on a friend and see if he can follow YOUR trail? Since he doesn't have any cat whiskers, he will have to pay close attention just by listening. OR you can have a friend put the blindfold on you and see if you can follow HIS trail. Just be careful where you leave your trail so neither of you will bump into anything. You might be surprised how much sharper your hearing gets when you REALLY pay attention.

Tooooo Loud!

Speaking of hearing and listening, did you know that very LOUD sounds can harm those delicate little parts in your ears that help you to hear? People who work near airplanes at airports or in construction jobs that use loud machinery or in factories where there is a lot of noise MUST wear special ear coverings to protect their hearing. If they didn't, they would lose that wonderful gift of sound.

But what about people who listen to loud MUSIC? They don't HAVE to listen to loud music like the people who have to work in noisy places but they do it anyway. AND some of them start to lose their hearing when they are still very young.

Music is one of the happy blessings of this world. Beautiful music can make you feel happy....patriotic music at a parade can make you feel proud of your country...soft, gentle music can help calm you down when you're upset...and a lullaby can even help you drift off to sleep. But very LOUD music can destroy delicate parts of your ear and take away your hearing. Did you know that? Will you be careful to stay far away from TOOOO LOUD noises of any kind—so you can save that great gift of sound that God gave you?? Please say yes.

Faith, Hope – and Charity!

Here are a few more names for the name game: Kevin means handsome, Ruth means kindness, Emily means an industrious one, Roy means king, Leo means lion, Alice means truthful, and Monica means one who gives advice.

All names are interesting but maybe the English have some of the most unusual ones. They have places with names like Wildboarclogh, Wormwood Scrubs, Harrow-on-the Hill, Saffron Walden, and Piddletrenthide. One of their popular cricket players was named Strangeways Pigg Strangeways and one of the heads of the Tetley Tea Company in London, England, was named Tetley Ironsides Tetley Jones. And in the nineteenth century there was an English couple whose third child was a son they named "And Charity" because they already had a daughter named Faith and another daughter named Hope!

You probably know what faith and hope mean but did you know that charity has several meanings? It can mean being generous enough to give money or food or clothes to the poor. It can mean being helpful and kind to anyone who is suffering in any way. And being charitable can also mean to give a person a second chance, to not make fun of somebody or not "judge" them to be guilty of something when you're not really sure they are. Do YOU have faith, hope—And Charity?

A Special Place

Do you know where you could find any of these things—apse, nave, narthex, vestibule, sanctuary? Have you ever SEEN any of those things? Well, sure you have—if you've ever been in a church. All of those are names for different parts of a church building!

If you know anyone who is an architect or an engineer, maybe they could explain to you where all those parts of a church are. Or maybe you could go to the library and look it up.

The last time you were in a church, what did you see? A Bible, candles, a songbook, maybe windows with colored glass? What else? How about people? People come together in a church to pray, to sing, to praise God. Do you do that when you're in a church? What DO you do when you're in a church?

117

A Close Shave!

Did you ever hear of the Great Sphinx of Gizeh? It's the most popular tourist attraction in Egypt and people travel from all over the world to see it. The Sphinx looks like the body of a lion with the head of a man! It was built about 5,000 years ago and is 66 feet tall—ten times taller than a very tall man! But what a lot of those tourists don't know is that the Sphinx is missing something!

When it was built, the lion-man also had a beard that was 3 feet long! It was a statue ten times taller than a very tall man with a beard ten times longer than a very long beard of a man! And guess what happened to the beard? Almost 200 years ago, way back in 1825, some explorers REMOVED the beard and took it to England to exhibit it in London's British Museum! So now the famous Sphinx is a statue with a close shave!

Did you ever see a man with a beard? Did you ever watch a man shave the beard from his face? Can you imagine someone shaving a beard off a huge statue? Maybe some day you will travel to Egypt to see the Sphinx—and you will be one of the tourists who knows that the giant Sphinx once had a giant beard!

There are so many amazing things to see in God's world that you could travel somewhere every day—by train, plane, bus, or balloon—and never see them all. Make a list today of all the things you would like to see and all the places where you would like to travel in God's amazing world.

Wanna Go to the Gobi?

Did you know that one of the largest deserts in the world is called the Gobi and its Chinese name is Sha-mo, which means "sand desert"—but there's not much sand IN this desert. It has fierce winds that have stripped away a lot of its sand so most of it is now bare rock!

You usually think of a desert being hot and dry all the time and the Gobi IS very hot in the summer but in the winter it gets very cold. It gets SO cold that the two-humped Bactrian camels who live there grow thick fur to keep them warm!

Everyone knows that a camel can live a long time without water, but did you know a rat can live even longer without water than a camel can? How long do you think YOU could live without water or anything to drink? The next time you get a nice cool drink of water, tell God thanks for water—and thanks for all the smart people who invented the thermos and other kinds of cans and bottles and other containers so you can take water with you wherever you go—even if you go to the Gobi!

The Alphabet Soup President

Did you know that the United States once had a president who people might have called "handicapped"—but nobody did. Franklin Delano Roosevelt was a smiling, vigorous man who looked as strong as an athlete, but he had had an illness called polio that paralyzed his legs and he wore two metal leg braces that weighed 60 pounds! That might have slowed down some people but this president was always busy starting new things. Some of the new programs he started were known by initials…the TVA, NRA, WPA…so some people laughingly called his programs "alphabet soup."

Later he was also known by HIS initials—FDR. He was ALSO known for the fact that he was so popular he was elected to four terms in the White House. He was the only president to ever be elected four times—and the only president who ever WILL be because there is now a rule that a president can only be elected for two terms.

In addition to the new programs he started, FDR also did a lot of other new things. He was the first president to travel by plane, the first president to appear on TV, and the first to appoint a woman to his Cabinet.

Did you ever know anyone who wore leg braces or used crutches or got around in a wheelchair? Some people have physical problems but lead busy, productive lives and some are so cheerful they set a good example for others—and isn't that great! And if you're friends with someone like that, aren't you lucky!

Wake Up! Wake Up!

Ring, ring…ding-a-ling. Sometimes bells can make beautiful music—like bicycle bells, church bells, or the bell on an ice-cream truck coming down the street to bring you a cool treat on a hot day. But an alarm clock bell might not sound so happy. It rings, rings to wake you up when you want to sleep, sleep. But wait! An alarm clock can be a happy sound too—when it wakes you up so you won't oversleep and be too late to take a trip to the zoo or the biggest baseball game of the year or maybe some day, a trip to the moon!

Isn't it great that God gave people the kind of brains that could come up with ideas for an alarm clock or an ice-cream truck or a space shuttle? What are some of your favorite inventions? Use your brain today to think of what kind of things you would like to invent some day. Then ask God to help you be "inventive!"

Sassafras and Sarsaparilla

Did you ever have a sarsaparilla with your peanut-butter sandwich? This was once a favorite carbonated drink that was sometimes pronounced "sassparilla," maybe because it's made with sassafras flavoring. And you may have had something very similar to drink because sassparilla tastes a lot like root beer! And that's because root beer is made from roots, herbs, and sarsaparilla!

Both the sarsaparilla and the sassafras are plants whose root bark has been used for many years to flavor beverages—or to make medicine or perfume. The sassafrass is an "understory" tree—which means it is one of the trees and shrubs that grow taller than the ground cover in a forest but not as tall as the large trees that form the "canopy" of the forest. And the sassafrass has four different kinds of leaves! One is egg-shaped, one has a three-finger shape, one is shaped like a left mitten, and one is shaped like a right mitten! What a tree! Hmmm…seems like this would be a good time for you to imagine you're in a forest, sitting under an understory tree, wearing your mittens and drinking a root-beer float…when along comes God and sits down beside you and he says… (Guess you'll have to finish this dream yourself!)

How Are You Like a Banana?

If you were going on a looooong trip like a safari or on a short trip like a bike ride, you might want to take along a snack. It could be something that tastes yummy, is good for you, and comes sealed airtight in its own package. How about a banana?!

When God made a banana, he "packaged" it in its own special "skin" so you don't have to wrap it up or seal it up in anything when you want to take it on a trip.

When God made you, he also "packaged" you in a special kind of skin, a skin that keeps YOU well-wrapped-up too!—but, unlike the banana, you DO have to add some clothes when you go on a long OR short trip.

Eat a banana today and think about where you might like to travel on a bike or on a safari…and tell God thanks for the special "packaging" he used when He made the banana AND you.

Mean Keen Jeans

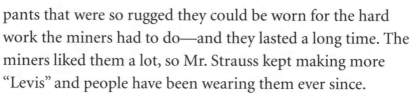

Hmmm...

Did you know that blue jeans almost became blue tents? Back in 1861, a man named Levi Strauss went to California with rolls of rugged blue material he was going to use to make tents for the gold miners who were camping there. But the miners told him what they really needed was some good sturdy trousers. So he used his tent material to make blue pants that were so rugged they could be worn for the hard work the miners had to do—and they lasted a long time. The miners liked them a lot, so Mr. Strauss kept making more "Levis" and people have been wearing them ever since.

At first, these pants were called Genoans because the rugged blue material Mr. Strauss used had been used by Italian sailors who were called Genoans—but the way the Americans pronounced the word, it sounded like "jeans" and that's what we call them today.

There are some tourist places today where you can "pan for gold" the way those early California miners did—so maybe you will wear your jeans and do that some day. But, for today, why don't you pan for gold by trying to think of all the things God made that are gold or yellow. You could start your list with the sun…or a boy with yellow hair…or???

Got a Second?

Did you know that Olympic champion Florence Griffith Joyner ran 100 meters in only ten and one-half SECONDS? And she ran 200 meters in 21.34 seconds. Both runs set a world record.

Did you know the very first Olympic games were held in Greece 700 years before Christ was born? They were held every four years for a long time until a Roman emperor put a stop to them. It was hundreds of years later before the games began again, again in Greece, in the year 1896. Now they are held in many different countries and people come from all over the world to participate. But it was not until 1912 that women—like Florence— were allowed to compete.

You can probably run very fast but not as fast as an Olympic champion. How fast can you run when it's time to go for an ice-cream treat or to go to your best friend's house to play? How fast can you run when someone needs help or when it's time to go to church or when you're asked to do a chore? Instead or running, do you sometimes say Wait a Second, Wait a Second….? Or do you try to run as fast as Florence Griffith Joyner?

What Is a High Wheel Ordinary?

It certainly doesn't LOOK ordinary but it WAS way back in the 1800s. The High Wheel Ordinary is a bicycle but not any kind you would see today—except maybe in a museum. This bicycle had one small wheel in the back and a tall, tall five-foot high wheel in the front. It must have not been TOO hard to ride because it was an "ordinary" kind of transportation for people at that time.

Things that were ordinary in the past seem funny to you today. But what do you think people of the future will think about today? Will they think 10-speed bikes are boring because they've invented rocket bikes? Will they think televisions and computers and cellular phones belong in a museum because they are so "old-fashioned?"

It's good to know that ONE thing will never change. God will still be there with you…to help you, to listen to you, to love you…today, tomorrow, and always!

A Prize-Winning Family

Do you know who was the first WOMAN to win the famous Nobel prize? Her name was Marie Curie. She and her husband, Pierre Curie, were French scientists who worked with dangerous radioactive material. They discovered two new elements—radium and polonium.

In 1903, the two Curies won a Nobel prize for their work in physics. Eight years later, in 1911, Marie won a second Nobel prize for her work in chemistry. And 23 years later, their daughter, Irene Joliot-Curie and her husband, Frederic Joliot-Curie, won the Nobel prize in chemistry. What a family!

Many "outstanding" people win prizes and become famous but did you know there are many people who never win any prizes but still do "outstanding" work—like firemen, teachers, doctors, school bus drivers, farmers, and especially mothers and fathers. How many outstanding people do you know?

Say a special prayer for one of them today.

A Presidential-Winning Family

Most families in the Unites States will never have a relative who is the country's president. But did you know there are some families who have had more than ONE president? John Adams was the second president and his son, John Quincy Adams, was the sixth. Benjamin Harrison was the twenty-third president and his grandfather, William Henry Harrison, was the ninth—and his great-grandfather was one of the men who signed the country's Declaration of Independence! Then there were the Roosevelts. Theodore Roosevelt was the twenty-fifth president and the thirty-first was also a Roosevelt. Franklin Roosevelt was only a distant cousin to Theodore but he had married Teddy's niece, Eleanor, so they were definitely relatives!

And then, by George, in 1989 George Herbert Walker Bush became the forty-first president and only eight years later, his son, George Walker Bush, became the forty-third president.

Do you think anyone in YOUR family will be president of the United States…or president of a company…or president of a baseball league…or president of a club…or president of a school's student council??? There are all KINDS of leaders. And they all need followers to get work done. Do you think you are a leader or a follower? Both are very important. God made both kinds—and he loves them all.

Can or CanNOT?

Did you know you canNOT lick your elbow? So if you accidentally dip it in chocolate sauce, you'll have to let your dog lick it off since you canNOT…but wait…chocolate is not good for dogs…so you might have to wash that elbow!

A crocodile canNOT stick out his tongue…so guess he canNOT lick his elbow either.

Pigs canNOT look up at the sky…so if you hear of a pig who saw a UFO, don't believe it.

An elephant canNOT jump…so he canNOT enter a jump rope contest.

A kagaroo CAN jump but he canNOT jump if his tail is lifted. He needs his tail to push off!

Well, these are just a few notes about NOTS.

What about YOU? What are the things that you canNOT do? And what are some of the things that you CAN do? If you make a list, you may be surprised to learn that there are LESS things you CAN- NOT do than the things you CAN!

Did You Notice?

Before a recent Super Bowl game, an eleven-year-old "reporter" asked one of the football "stars" a question. She asked, "How many laces does an NFL regulation football have?" He didn't know! Then she asked several other star players the same question. None of them knew! Do you know?

While the grown-up reporters were asking the players questions about their game plan and technical things about their training, she asked some other interesting questions, like which player had the stinkiest locker! And they answered her questions.

Now in case you didn't know, there are eight laces on the football. And this shows how easy it is to NOT notice things that are in your everyday life. How many hundreds of times those players had held a football in practice or in professional games—but they never noticed the laces. And the laces in a football are necessary and so they are important.

In the same way, some people go through every day and never notice some of the important things in their house or school or church. Yet other people are "in-takers"...they notice everything...they take in everything they see AND they remember it.

Which one are you? Which one would you like to be?

A Birdbrain!

If you call somebody a birdbrain, you're insulting them, saying you think they are stupid! But wait! A birdbrain must be pretty smart since a bird can fly by itself, but a person needs an airplane to fly! And some birds can sing soooo much better than some people.

Have you ever seen one of those cute little yellow canaries? They are great singers. When they are baby birds and just start to make little noises, they are a lot like little babies just starting to make goo-goo, gurggling sounds. BUT by the time a canary is eight months old, it can sing like an adult. And a baby can't sing or even talk by that age.

And did you know that canaries sing a lot in the spring but then, in the summer, when they shed their feathers, they seem to shed their songs too! By the next spring, they've learned to sing NEW songs! That's pretty smart for a teeny little yellow bird.

So maybe when you call somebody a birdbrain, you're giving them a compliment! But they probably won't know that so you better NOT call anyone a birdbrain. Instead, try to think of some people you don't like very much and give them a nice compliment. Tell them you think they are smart or neat or a good ball player or a good singer. It will make them feel good—and it might make you feel good too.

Using Your Noodle

When you eat supper tonight, would you like to have butterflies, shells, thimbles, ribbons, or radiators? What? You don't want to eat any of those things? Well, you MIGHT like them—if you like pasta!

You've probably eaten spaghetti and meatballs but did you know that spaghetti is the Italian word for "a length of cord"? So you ate cord and meatballs! And there are lots of other interesting Italian names for different shapes of pasta. For example, *farfalle* (fahr-FAH-lay) is Italian for butterflies—so you may LIKE to have butterfly-shaped pasta for supper!

Sometimes macaroni and cheese is made with pasta that looks like little shells and the Italian name for shells is

conchiglie (kohn-CHEE-lyuh). Then there's *ditalini* (dih-tah-LEE-nee) which is Italian for little thimbles. And fettuccine (feht-tuh-CHEE-nee) is Italian for little ribbons. If you ever ate fettucine, did you notice the noodles look like little ribbons?

Maybe you might even like to have radiators for dinner if you have radiatore (rah-dyah-TOH-reh) which is a ruffled, ridged pasta that looks like the old-fashioned radiators that were once used to heat many homes—and still are used in some homes today.

There are lots of other pastas that have Italian names to fit the shapes of spirals, wagon wheels, quills, and small mustaches!

So the next time you have some funny-shaped pasta, you can surprise your friends by telling them you ate butterflies or wagon wheels or mustaches for dinner! And when you say the Blessing before dinner, you can tell God thanks for shells and thimbles and ribbons and radiators AND for the people who invented spaghetti!

Did You Ever See a Moonbow?

You may have seen a rainbow—that beautiful colorful arch that sometimes appears in the sky after a rainstorm—but did you know there is also something called a moonbow?

You have to be at a special place at a special time to see this very special sight. You could go to Victoria Falls in Africa OR you could go to Cumberland Falls in Kentucky. Not too many people have seen moonbows because they only appear a few times each year—always by a huge waterfall on a clear evening with a full moon.

Most moonbows are white but when there's a lot of water coming over the waterfall and the moon is very bright, moonbows can have brilliant red and violet colors.

Would you like to see a moonbow some time? Do you like to watch for a rainbow after the rain? Isn't it fun that God put so many surprises for you on the land, in the sea, and even in the sky?

The United States Camel Corps?

Before the Army had trucks or tanks or airplanes or jeeps, they had to use horses or mules to move people and equipment. And some of those horses and mules were used by the Army out west where it was very hot and dry. Then one day, someone got the idea that maybe CAMELS would work better than horses and mules since camels usually live in a hot, dry desert. So the Army ordered thirty-two camels to be sent on a three-month ocean voyage from Egypt to Texas!

When the camels went to work, the officer in charge was so impressed that he put in an order for MORE camels. And some of those camels were used when the Army surveyed a route from New Mexico to California, trailblazing part of what became the famous highway known as Route 66.

Three camels could carry as much equipment on their backs as six mules could pull in a wagon. AND the camels could move twice as fast. So the Camel Corps seemed like a good idea.

BUT the camels did NOT make friends fast. They ate everything—including Army tents. They were stubborn and bad-tempered and hard to handle. Sometimes they got mad at the soldiers and when they got mad, they got even. The camels would bite or spit or step on somebody's foot!

So in 1863, when the good idea had turned into a bad problem, the Army auctioned off the camels—and that was the end of the United States Camel Corps.

Would you like to have a camel for a friend—a friend who gets mad and pouts and sulks or bites or spits or steps on your foot? Maybe nobody ever taught the camel that that is not a polite or good way to act so the camel doesn't know any better. But YOU know better, don't you?

A Singing Whale?

Did you know that if you could go waaaay out into the ocean and drop a microphone deep down, you just might hear a strange "singing" sound—the song of a whale! These huge swimmers can't make signs to one another because it's too dark to see way down in the depths of the ocean so they use sounds to communicate and to tell one another where to find food. And guess what? Their songs sound a bit like today's electronic music! Now isn't that a whale of a story!

Maybe some day you'll see a TV show starring a singing whale—or maybe not. Would YOU like to be a star on TV? What would you do—sing a song, dance a dance, tell a funny story? When you grow up, who knows where God might like you to go. You could be on TV or sailing on the ocean looking for whales or maybe being a teacher, a doctor, a butcher, a baker, or a candlestick-maker. Which do you think it will be?

Last Name Game

You've heard what some FIRST names mean, but what about some LAST names? Originally, most last names were actually the names of the kind of work the person did, like Mr. Farmer or Mr. Hunter or Mr. Baker or Mr. Cook. Mr. Schumacher was probably a shoemaker who made shoes for people and Mr. Smith was probably a blacksmith who made shoes for horses! Sometimes they were the names of the kind of place the person came from like Dr. Woods or Mr. Park. They may have come from a relationship like Mr. Stevenson who was Steven's son or Dr. Johnson who was John's son. Or they could have been a description like Mr. Young or Mr. Moody or Mr. Witt who told funny stories. Through the years, names got changed and spelled diffcrently and today it's hard to tell WHERE those names came from!

Can you guess where YOUR name came from? Do you like your last name— or your first name or your nickname? If you don't have a nickname, would you like to have one? You COULD make up one for yourself. But whether you use your last name, first name, or nickname, God will still know who you REALLY are—because he made you and he's your best friend!

there goes Mr. Cook...

Have You Ever Heard of Sisu?

This is a word you MAY never hear because it's a word used in Finland and it means different things to different people. It can mean having the courage to work hard at something you believe in even when others discourage you— or it can describe a great work of art that is simple yet wonderful. And there's an example of "sisu" that is one of the great wonders of the United States. It's the St. Louis Gateway Arch—a simple but amazing steel arch that stands at the edge of the great Mississippi River and soars high into the sky. Tourists come from all over the world to see it.

This "sisu" piece of architecture was designed by a man from Finland named Eero Saarinen and, like the sisu word, it is different at different times—brilliant when the sun flames off its sides, shadowy in the moonlight, and sometimes almost disappearing in the morning mists. The Arch is a reminder that St. Louis was the Gateway to the West way back when people came to this city in covered wagons or steamships, courageously setting out to explore America's western world of cowboys and Indians and buffalo and prairies.

Some people thought those pioneers were crazy to head out into an unknown territory. Some people thought Saarinen's design of this towering arch was so unusual it could never be built.

And so today, this "wonder" is a monument to the pioneers and to the architect—a symbol that with imagination, courage and hard work, anything and everything is possible.

Do you know anyone who has sisu—someone who may not be a movie star or a sports hero but IS a good person who lives simply and works quietly and has the courage to be true to what he or she believes? Would you like to be that kind of person?

If you ever get a chance to see the Gateway Arch and ride to the top in the little train that is INSIDE the tall arch, look out at the Mississippi River and think about the pioneers and the architect and sisu.

With And Without

Did you know there is a very big saltwater lake that is named the Dead Sea? Most lakes have lots of fish and underwater plants living in them, but this lake has water that is sooo salty, NOTHING can live in it—and that's why it got the name Dead Sea.

Sigh! I wish I had a horse.

The Dead Sea is a lake without life. A dead pan is a face without a smile or frown or ANY expression. A dead head is someone who got free tickets to the ball game without paying for them. And a dead letter is one without the right address so it can't get delivered.

All those "dead" things are without—except for the dead head who is happy WITH those baseball tickets!

Do you ever have a day when you feel totally without? Without fun, without friends, without pizza, without zip-a-dee-do-dah? Well, everybody has a day like that once in awhile. But what about the WITH days? Do you have days with fun, with friends, with pizza, and maybe even with baseball tickets? Try to use those boring dead days, the withouts, to find a nice quiet spot and just sit and visit with God and think about all those ALIVE, with, zip-a-dee-do-dah days…and say thanks.

Trees With Antifreeze?

You probably know that cars need gas and water in them to run and people need blood in them to keep their hearts pumping so THEY can run. But did you know that trees have a liquid in them too and it's called tree sap? This liquid feeds the trees and helps them grow.

But, since it's a liquid, the sap could freeze if the winter was VERY cold—and that might kill a tree. So what's a tree to do?

To keep warm, people can wear lots of heavy clothes and eat hot soup and drink hot drinks. And cars have owners who can take them to a service station and fill them with antifreeze so their liquids won't freeze. But what about a tree? Well, God took care of that!

When God made trees, he put a reminder in their memory bank so that every year when the weather starts getting cold, that's a signal for the trees to stop growing and then shed all their leaves. Since the trees don't have to feed the leaves anymore, the tree sap changes and turns into a "magic" fluid that acts just like a car's antifreeze!

Isn't it great the way God thought of everything when he made the world? He made SOME bushes and trees—like Christmas trees— so they could stay green all year. But when he made shade trees that lose their leaves, God provided antifreeze!

Could You Be a Witworm?

If you look in your dictionary, you might not find this word because it's a very old word that meant "someone who enjoys wit." And what is wit? It can mean humor, comedy, anything that makes you laugh or the power to make someone else laugh.

You've probably heard the word "bookworm" and know that means somebody who really really likes to look at and collect and read books. So, since you are reading this book, maybe you are a bookworm—and since this book is supposed to be full of fun or wit, maybe you ARE a witworm!

Of course, a wit can also mean someone who God gave a sense of humor, imagination, and intelligence. Oh, yes, you must definitely be a witworm!

Last Page

This may be the last page but it is NOT THE END. This book includes just a FEW of the oodles of fun facts found in God's wonderful world of wonders. There are lots and lots more, just waiting for you to find them. Start to NOTICE, read books, listen to what other people say, and pay attention to what you see wherever you go. You'll find that learning facts is more than an education—facts are fun! Soooo....

What is your favorite fun fact from this book?

_____

_____

What is your favorite fun fact from some other book?

_____

_____

Where is the best place to look for facts?

_____

_____

Where is the best place to have fun?

_____

_____

Who do you know who knows the most facts?

_____

_____

Who do you know who is the most fun?

_____

_____

When is the best time to look for fun facts?

_____

_____

How many fun facts do you think there are in the world?

_____

_____

**If you would like to find more fun facts,
look for the other "Fun Facts" books in this series.**